Things I Needed To Say

Poetic Conversations

By Monica Lee and Jørgen Panduro

MIX
Papir fra ansvarlige kilder
Paper from responsible sources
FSC® C105338

Monica Lee and Jørgen Panduro

Things I Needed To Say

Poetic Conversations

Books on Demand GmbH, Copenhagen,

Denmark

Cover: Idea, Jørgen Panduro - Graphics, Jimmy Machon

Publisher: Books on Demand GmbH, Copenhagen, Denmark

Print: Books on Demand GmbH, Norderstedt, Deutschland

ISBN: 9788743029120

I fell in love with "true love" when I was 5 years old.
Little did I know "true love" was 5, 287 miles away.
Monica

This book is dedicated to the lonely, the shy, the lost, the broken, the heart broken, the rejected, the abandoned, the thrown away, the hopeless, the hopeful, the dreamers, the lovers and everyone else in between - don't give up and always say the things you need to say.

About the authors

Monica Lee

Monica is a Relationship/Intimacy Coach, Sex Educator/ Advocate, writer, Tantra Educator, Public Speaker, Host and Creator of Front Porch Sex Talk with Monica Lee and a nurse.

She has clients all over the world that she speaks to and helps them connect with themselves and their partners on a deeper level of cosmic bliss through her practice The Art of Sensual Being.

Her Podcast, Front Porch Sex Talk with Monica Lee reaches millions of people all over the world as she speaks about dating, love, intimacy, relationships, divorce, sexual health and dysfunctions, sex over 65, and tantra.

She currently lives in Texas with her sidekick Pitbull, George and where she is known to her friends and family as the Moon Goddess driving her jeep and walking barefoot at midnight sipping her sweet tea!

For more visit monicalee.me

Jørgen Panduro has a Master's Degree (MBC) Master's in Business Coaching with specialty in Protreptic which is an old Greek art of conversation through concepts.

Jørgen is the author of the books:

Pan Poetica (ISBN: 978-87-4302-709-6) with the subtitle "Betydningens digte" which is translated into meaningful poems.
It *is a collection of poems mainly written in Danish, but there are 11 poems written in English, 2 in German and 1 in Swedish.*

Meaningful poems (ISBN: 978-87-4302-949-6) with the subtitle "Pan Poetica" which is a collection of poems written in English.

Content

Introduction

Have you ever wanted to speak your heart and yet you just couldn't get the words out? Or you thought, "I don't want to lose a friendship or what if I scare them off?" Because let's face it -sometimes we can say things that scares the hell out of people. Maybe it is because we think it could be too soon to have such in depth conversations or sometimes.... just maybe the other person is not on the same level as you and is not ready to go to such depths.

Well - let me tell you, I have never had that problem. Speaking my mind has never been an issue for me especially when it comes to me speaking my heart. I always knew that when it was time the right person would not be afraid of my words but embrace them. I was always told that I was "intimidating", "too passionate", "too intense", "too much this or too much that". I refused to be anything less as I knew that it would shortchange the one that was out there for me.

As a Relationship/Intimacy Coach, Sex Educator, Tantra Practitioner, and Radio Show Host, I interact with quite a few people that have a hard time talking about their issues and matters of the heart. So many times, I have worked with clients that communication was an issue because they could not say the things they wanted to say. I would sit and listen to them and be the one to mediate, help them open, and truly say what they felt. It can be quite difficult to open and be vulnerable to speak those things. It is important to speak your heart as we may never have that opportunity again. Plus, what if... what if the other person was too shy. And so, what if you say things and they run. It just means that they were not the one for you. Never dim your light so others can be comfortable.

So, let me tell you all about this little girl at the age of 5 years old. She was so in awe of love. She was actually "in love" with love. You are probably thinking, what does she know at the age of 5 about love...yeah, I know! Well, she knew that she loved and wanted a strong man that would keep her safe, protect her, make her laugh, wear a black leather jacket and most of all love her.

She knew that somewhere out there her strong man was waiting for her. Little did she know he was 5,287 miles away and she would not meet him for another 41 years... but hey what are a few miles and a few years huh? I mean seriously when it comes to the love of your life, that means nothing. The heart does not measure time, distance, or language.

So, let's fast forward 41 years to when she is 46, to November 22-2019. And in case you did not know...that little girl is me. I had just turned 46 the month before in October. I was living my life in such a way that I was putting out the vibe of love, peace and creating my own happily ever after, as I was single. Although I was not giving up on the possibility of a relationship, I just wasn't focused on it, but left that door open to The Universe. I knew every night when I walked at midnight that I would speak my heart to the moon as she was and is my best friend. I would speak to her about this man that I did not know existed...maybe he did, maybe he didn't. I took comfort in pouring my heart out to her and knowing that as cheesy as this sounds, that he was out there under the same moon as me.

On March 6th, 2006, my ex-husband and I decided that we would split, and that very night I started writing a love letter to a man that I didn't know...like I said...did he even exist? Was he a figment of my imagination? Everything I had stored up in my heart I poured on to the pages...some tear stained pages, some pages that went on and on telling of my day and the plans of the future if we ever found each other, and on other days it was just a sentence...."Where are you? I need you so much today...I can't breathe without you!". I already loved his man and missed him, and I didn't even know who or where he was.

November 22, 2019 I was minding my own business on social media when one of my friends posted something and I saw this beautiful soul. My heart stopped for a brief moment, my spirit jumped, and my soul came to a screeching halt and said" That's him!!". I clicked on his name and looked at his profile - I had to know him, my heart was racing, I was breathless. His eyes in his profile picture literally hooked me. It wasn't the color, but the soul I saw that spoke to me. My soul knew his soul...perhaps I was his before in another time, but I knew that I knew we had been "One" at one time. It felt like when you are walking, not really paying attention, then you bump into someone and you cosmically collide.... yeah, that was us.

So, as I clicked his profile, I saw that he was from Denmark... WHAT...DENMARK!?! I live in Texas. Yup, I googled the miles right then and there. 5, 287 miles but hey, no biggie that is what airplanes are for. I immediately clicked "Add Friend". I thought 41 years to meet him was a long time, but it was those moments waiting for him to accept my request that lasted what seemed like a lifetime. I kept going back to see if he had cancelled the request or if it was still pending. BOOM... HE ACCEPTED! If I could have done cartwheels, I would have.... but um, yeah instead I screamed a bit and sighed a deep sigh of relief. He was going to realize he loved me at some point. Notice

I said, "realize" meaning he already loved me but did not even know it yet. (That is what I keep telling him even to this day). Now that he accepted my friendship, now what? I had to tell him that he was the one my soul has been looking for, waiting for, aching to be with. One small issue though - How do you say those things within the first 90 seconds of a new friendship without looking like an idiot? I sit here and laugh because it took another 6 months for that to happen... more on that later.

I tried to message him from time to time, but he was shy and not very conversational, even though he does not lack words. I knew I was not going to give up on him. I would wait for him another 41 years if I had to...although one day I said, "Hey, we can have tacos and great conversation if I ever make it to Denmark" in which he replied "I don't like tacos". I was crushed, heartbroken because those that know me, know that I love my tacos, but I would have gladly given them up just to be with him. That would have been hard, but he was and is totally worth it.

We laugh about it now because on one of his comments on a post of mine he quoted a lyric from a song "I'd sell my soul for you babe" (again he loved me already and didn't know it yet). So our joke is I would give up tacos for you which is kind of like selling your soul. Our messages remained short, sweet and one liners. I was not giving up on him.... he is my warrior, and a goddess does not give up on her warrior.

Things took a change on April 4th, 2020 at 2:33 pm. I was in my 90 days of quarantine doing my daily videos and he commented on it. Immediately I messaged him. We chatted briefly and he asked for my phone number. I did not hesitate; I gave it to him and within seconds Depeche Mode Enjoy The Silence was playing on my phone...my ringtone. I looked at it and Denmark was calling me. I answered and said, "Hello darling" - I was not fully prepared to hear the voice on the other end of the line. When I heard his voice that was it. He took my breath away; quite sure I had an orgasm.... the sound of his voice was so familiar to me. I melted and felt so comfortable with him. My heart finally felt whole again. We spoke for a while and had quite a bit in common. I found out he, among other things was writing poetry and I told him I was a writer. I read a piece that I had written a very long time ago back in 2006 right about the time I started my nightly love letters. It was called "Crimson Tears". I always knew that when the right person read those words or heard them that he would be the one. Many have read them, heard them, but nobody reacted like he did.

We said our goodbyes and I was lost. Now that I knew he existed; I was scared I would never hear from him again. The next day, I woke up to a beautiful poem called "Crimson Tears". I could not believe my eyes, I kept reading it over and over again wanting so badly for those words to be for me, about me. If I had that page in my hands the ink would have worn off from me reading it so much and crying. Those words in response to my piece of writing sealed the deal. I was already in love with him, but those words sealed the deal for me. I was not just in love, I was madly, truly, deeply in love with him.

After a few calls with him face to face, I started to pour my heart out and tell him Things I Needed To Say. He lives in Denmark, I live in Texas, there is a global pandemic going on and I did not know if I was ever going to get to see him. I could not stay quiet. I needed him to know that he was my Cosmic Supernova, my Warrior. I needed him to know that even across the ocean and through the miles I was in love with him. I needed him to know all these things. I wrote "How", and he responded with his poem to me. This went on and on with our poetic conversations and each one more and more intense. More and more passionate.

What you are about to read in this book is a love story that is so beautiful that we wanted to give hope to others. Long distance relationships are hard especially when you are on lock down and can't travel.

We wanted to show the world that no matter the distance and even in a pandemic that you can find the love of your life. The words you are going to read are the Things I Needed To Say to him and his responses to me in Poetic Conversations. This is a cosmic love story that happens when you trust The Universe and the Sacred Contracts come to be…but you also have to trust the internet to not go down so you can have your virtual dates and conversations. Welcome to dating in 2020!

As you read this, you are reading my very vulnerable words, my charismatic spirit and deeply passionate heart. I am baring my soul to him and allowing you to see how liberating and freeing it can be when you speak your heart. You will see his responses so strong and powerful to cradle me and keep me safe, to reassure me, and to love me. We are both very bold spirits with quite different styles, but we complement each other in such a ying and yang way that it truly is "cosmic". I let the words ooze from my spirit, dripping with passion and intensity then he comes back with poetic beauty pouring from his spirit to create "our" story.

So many times, couples are scared to speak about certain topics and in this book, we have conversations about that and so much more.

This book is divided into 2 parts; "Poetic Longings and Meaningful Conversations". You will see that we are quite different, but on the same path. My words are wild like paint splattered on a canvas with brush strokes everywhere and he comes in to polish it up to show our true ebb and flow where we complement each other in all that we say. You are going to read the love story of Monica and Jørgen and how the goddess and her warrior say the things they need to say.

Monica

I did not know

Wondering around searching for love

not in a hurry and no prayers to the non-exiting above

I was happy but still missed – you know

Little did I know when she appeared

short innocent conversations but still not cleared

There was something but I guess I had to see it grow

With a poem I responded to "Crimson Tears"

suddenly it was if we had been lovers for years

I never thought that love would overflow

Since then our existence has extended

the love we have is transcended

Seen in the dark – I guess it will glow

Jørgen

Part 1

Poetic longing

Prelude

Monica

When I met Jørgen and started to talk to him, there were so many things I wanted to tell him that was coming from a very deep place in my heart, my mind, and my soul. Truly, it is an intense longing to be in front of him to say these words. So many times we just can't speak our heart, but I let it all out.

Through the miles I cried, whispered, screamed, laughed, had quite a few orgasms as these things I needed to say were coming from me. Longing to be next to him is an understatement.

What can I say, we are in the middle of a pandemic and as much as I wish I was holding his hand, caressing his face, sitting next to him, baring my soul with these words I am putting them here. I am hoping to give others inspiration that no matter what is happening, you can always speak your heart.

Jørgen

When I respond to Monica´s outburst from her heart, mind, and soul, you will find my answers to be in a poetic form, and that each and every one of them is coming from my heart, mind and soul as well. I chose a poetic form because the lyrics can reach another dimension when you are able to put the subject into a world where rhymes, syntax, words, metaphors, analogies, and concepts can transcend the view into a new perspective.

Crimson Tears

Monica

The heart knows what the soul feels.... what the mind seeks.
True love.... the kind of love that transcends time.... realities.... worlds.
The kind of love that binds hearts...souls... that even though lifetimes pass....it is always remembered.
I say this because I remember you.
I ache for you, my darling, as I always do...as I always have.
My tears are so painful they are crimson in color...the color of my bleeding heart.
Why...why can I not have peace enough to have you for a whole lifetime.
Why...why must you always be taken from me?
Is fate this cruel to us that it laughs at my tears.... the tears I cry for you.
Or is it that our love is so pure....so rare...that others curse us for they want it for themselves...yet cannot have.
My darling, beloved....do you not hear me...do you not hear me calling your name as I wander this earth.... searching for you.... crying for you.
Do you not see me in the crowds, my love, my face is smeared with crimson tears for you.
Can you not see how I ache for your soul to embrace me?

Do you feel me?
I reach out in the darkness...only to embrace the night...empty.
The wolves.... they cry.... are they crying with me or is it their conspiracy laugh along with fate...mocking me... torturing us?
I long for your touch, my skin hurts...it is your touch that shall heal me.
I crave your love, it is my life force.
I thirst for your kiss.... because of it I exist......feed me.... I beg you...feed me your spirit...give me life....my darling.
Lifetime after lifetime it is always the same....I find you, only for you to be taken from me....once again....ripped from my life....without reason...without cause....leaving me lying in the street in the puddle of my crimson tears.
Another lifetime passes I search feverishly.... I find you....and you are taken...not mine to have.
And so, I wait.... watching.... the love you share with another.
Again...my trail of crimson tears stains the streets.
She has your love...and yet when our eyes meet.... our hearts know.... what our souls feel...what our minds seek.
But again, fate has other plans....so I travel again...another life.
This pain my heart cannot take....my face remains stained from the tears.

Wandering as always...restless through the lands...with no apparent direction...only the scent of your soul to follow and the ache of my soul to lead.
How will I know I am where I am to be?
I will know because at first sight....our souls will intertwine...and as we lay next to each other...finally...finally...we have peace...and sleep....will no longer be a fantasy...but our dreams will be as one...our movements in unison...a beautiful erotic dance...of our spirits.
My body cannot go on.... spent from my journeys.... devoured by pain.... yet consumed by you, my beloved.
Time after time...life after life...my heart knows what my soul feels...what my mind seeks.
Come to me my love.... come to me so that your kiss may quench my thirst
Come to me my darling so that your touch will heal my soul....and your love will awaken me.
Come to me...wake me from my hell.... save me.... what you have the power to awaken...no one...not anything can put back to sleep.
And you, my love...my darling...it is you...I shall forever live through and live forever for.
I am yours...I belong to you and you alone.......wipe my crimson tears away.... give me peace...
Stay with me.... I beg you.
Come to me my love.... come to me....

Crimson tears running slowly down my cheek
it´s the love from you I seek
where are you – you hold my soul
I´m trembling, I shiver – you have control

My heart is pulsating, and my crimson tears
color my spirit - when will you be near

close against my body – a gentle touch
wherever you are, I need you so much

In despair I search my soul and the light
thinking of you and hold us so tight
our naked bodies in ecstatic exploration
they magnetize, they sparkle with no hesitation

Where are you my darling? I want you in me
Without your energy I cannot be

My crimson tears hold you dear –

How

Monica

How.... How can I not be consumed with you? When immediately I felt like I have touched your face with my fingertips as they still ache from tracing your lips.

How can my thoughts not constantly be of you? Because the moment we connected it felt as if you had already been part of me at one time....as though I miss you.

How can I not want just one chance with you? Even to spend 5 minutes in your presence would be a lifetime of bliss.

But.... how could I not want more of you? To look into your eyes, to feel the depth of your soul, to feel your fingertips electrically on my skin, to feel the warmth of your breath on my face.... your sweet lips against mine.

How could I be so selfish to wish with everything in me that we were right next to each other and the ocean did not separate us? Because instantly, I felt such a peace with you that took away any fear I have ever felt. Because instantly I felt like you have protected me before and comforted me. Because you give me a feeling of "Home". Because in your embrace is where I know I belong....it all feels so familiar, YOU feel so familiar. Perhaps that is why your arms are what I pay attention to, I have felt them before.

How could I not be breathless at the sight of you? When your soul spoke to mine before words were ever uttered. And the sound of your voice echoes in my spirit. You took my breath away then….and even after hearing you…. you take my breath away now.

How do I face the realization that miles are between us, because when I close my eyes, I picture you next to me….I picture you dancing with me in the kitchen…I picture you holding me….kissing me…making love to me. Because when I close my eyes, I imagine us laughing and listening to music…. having deep and meaningful conversation while I steal a kiss from you occasionally, as I would not be able to resist. Because when I close my eyes, I am sitting on the couch and I am watching you write your poems…the look on your face….the concentration…and once again, you take my breath away.

How can I stay away and look in another direction, not at you? Because when I look at you even behind the screen…. I see a beautiful soul, with a beautiful heart with a beautiful mind. I see a man that captivates me, has me completely mesmerized.

How can I not reach out to you? Because my soul aches to feel your soul...to hear your words...to see you smile...because all that makes my day. I have tasted your essence and I crave you...I crave more.
How can the most amazing man be the sweetest perfection and take my breath away all at the same time.... Because he is Jørgen...

The "how" is your urge and catalyst
It´s within but it´s not there, because you´re past the "how" you just used
I hear your "how" and see through it – I´m your agonist
In the separation, the craving and longing amplifies and it´s confused

It´s the sound of the heart – here the longing cries

Your "how" is now – it´s real
The future is the past when we create the present
the present does not exist – and the "how" is gone with none – it´s surreal
we are extending - reaching out, but we are not disoriented

It´s the sound of the heart – here the mind tries

My darling - you should touch my lips and feel my arms
Your mind is so expressive, it´s alluring – stretch charms
Waiting is a virtue; love is epic, and feelings are vivid
No matter the distance or the obstacles our love is transmitted

It´s the sound of the heart – here love thrives

Breathless

Monica

After speaking to him... as I am about to hang up and say..."See you later my darling"...my throat grows tight, my chest hurts, my lungs feel as if they will collapse....I am breathless, I panic because the most natural thing to do is to breathe...and I feel like the next breath is not there for me to take....the screen is blank.

I tell him...." I feel like I cannot breathe" ...a deep ache grips me, and the tears fall uncontrollably.

He tells me....
"Breathe me in and feel my soul melting with yours"
And in that moment.... a deep breath came to me, my Beloved in true form rescued me, once again, for I am truly living on your breath....

Jørgen

Let me be your in-spiration – inhale my spirit with your love
respirate – slowly inhale, exhale, and feel my energy
bringing your inner emotions to live with me in synergy
calibrate your heartbeat and breath with mine and feel the cosmic love from above

I Am In Love With Him

Monica

Many people can say that they love someone. Love can be different for many as it could be love for people, places, and things, not to mention different levels, degrees, intensities.
There are those that walk this earth and can honestly say that they are "In Love" - I am one of those people.

In my 46 almost 47 years of life...I can say that I am finally in love...madly, truly.... cosmically in love.
I know I am in love with him because my heart aches in his absence....though they say "absence makes the heart grow fonder".....that phrase means nothing to me as my love is immense for him....and his absence leaves me paralyzed.
No, no, no....again, I say, that phrase means nothing to me because you see.....my love for him, my beautiful "184",....how can I say that his absence would make me grow fonder, because he is part of me...a part that I never want to be without!
My heart knows the difference between loving and being in love....and my heart is in love with his...because it was created to beat just for him.

He is my gift from The Universe...how could I not be in love with this beautiful Star.
We came from such a faraway place to finally meet.
To not love him would be a tragedy...truly a life of loss, but....to love him, my pleasure, my honor....to be in love with him....is to finally, fully live!
There is no doubt....I know I am in love with him, as I close my eyes all I can see is our travels, our conversations, our quiet times, the laughs, tears, the nights of love making only 2 people in love can share...the passion...intimacy of his arms around me just holding me and his words to fill my spirit....the safety of his soul protecting mine and mine protecting his.....the books....our flowing of creativity merging through time.....our endless journey together as our faces become lined with age....and our hands even in our 90s still clasp to one another...and my eyes whether they are 46 or 96 are only for my true love...my Jørgen...

Jørgen

My darling
I´ve been absent from you my whole life, and I´m still absent in the current presence
In virtuality we meet with laughter, tears, and intense gazes through the screen of fluorescence
For now, with all our dreams is just a temporary

acceptance

Our first meeting will be a return – a rendez vous of lost spirits in the lights
Virtue of reality and dreams, no matter how hard it seems within sights
The things we want to do constitutes our affection, and takes us to new heights

I Need

Monica

I need to hold you

I need you to hold me back

I need to kiss you and you kiss me back

I need to look into your eyes and see myself in your thoughts.

I need to tell you how much I miss you, and I need to hear you tell me I am not crazy.

I need to watch you sleep at night so I can drift off to sleep in the peace of your presence

I need to have you next to me, because I feel I cannot breathe until you are with me.

I need to tell you how in love I am with you, because my heart feels like it will explode unless I speak those words.

I need.... you...my beloved, Jørgen...only you!

My dear

You can´t need what you already have – open your eyes

search your soul – feel your heart, make a sigh

I´m there in your sleep, in your kiss and hugs - oh my

You do not even have to think twice

Your need is merely a beautiful longing for proximity

Me in your thoughts is a reflection, of your feelings

I mirror you in aesthetic love and sublimity

Whispers

Monica

The Goddess:

I want to be next to you....so I can wake up and tell you "I love you" as you sleep....so when you dream, you'll dream of my love for you.

The Warrior:

"I would love to have you next to me and feel your gentle touch and silent whisper."

Jørgen

Silent messages, in between lines
the conversation in the conversation those are the signs

The gentle touch is a whisper, the dream is mute when it moans
The "laying" next to me is a poem read loud and caress your erotic zones

I whisper – I will take you to states of pleasure where you tremble like a leaf
until you uncontrollably come in an explosion beneath me, and come to yourself in relief

Only You

Monica

Only you...Only you can embrace my soul the way you do
Only you can kiss my spirit and lift me up
Only you can breathe into my heart to make it beat
Only you can speak to my mind

It is in your arms where I am loved
It is you that I love.... only you

Jørgen

Lonely you will never be
Lonely in the world and life – no because you´ve got me
Lonely at heart and soul – you will not feel
Lonely when you speak is no conversation to whom you will kneel

It is you I will caress
It is you I will undress

In A Dream

Monica

I have heard his voice call out to me in the dark...it echoes deeply in my soul.

But....

I have yet to feel his touch...yet my skin misses his fingertips.

I have not felt his lips...yet my lips ache for his...as if I have felt them before...and the taste of what remains has me missing his kiss

Dreams -

the stretched mind, the playground of thoughts, escapism of suppressed feelings.

Seems -

to be reality on a high dose of caffeine – you are shaking, but your awareness is raised

Means -

nothing and everything you want them to be, just remember to translate the faith at the gate.

Memes -

your dreams circulate around specific senses – you must interpret the underlying themes.

Genes -

if dreams have genes, we will share the same DNA of which love is built and we are filled

Teens -

like young at hearts we will kiss, and the touch of our lips will radiate taking our souls to another state we create

Pan dreams

What Forever Looks Like

Monica

I look in his eyes and know that I just want to be there forever…. I love how I look in the reflection of his eyes. The reflection of me is his Goddess…. even when I am not donning the red lips, he still sees me…and the same look shows in his eyes.

I could see his love for me in his eyes even before he said the words…. I walk through those doors to his soul and forever want to stay.
I stand next to him and just know that I never want to leave his side.
I look up at him because I am fucking short and feel his energy envelope me, wrapping me up in his safety forever.

I kiss him…and forever want his lips to have mine…anytime he wants.
My kisses are forever only his.

So as the tears flow thinking of him as he is not near me…..I want to fast forward time so that it will go by quickly….so that I can hold my Viking in my arms in my forever.

If ever comes before always, then forever will have no infinity
Our love is extended beyond eternity and has no time aspect
it is the moment that has passed, and lives in the future that constitutes our affinity

I will hold you and look at you while my eyes glare, your red lips
they are so vivid, alluring and inviting to be kissed
Your lips have their own language, speaking the words of your soul – it´s a fix.

Sweet spot

Monica

As he slides his hands over my body...I am lost in that moment...gasping for air...needing his touch as if it is the only thing keeping me alive.

His hands reaching that sweet spot where he knows I melt every time....before he lets me have that deep release....where he creates my pleasure....he whispers...."And who does this belong to??

Between breaths...begging him with my eyes to take me...I whisper..." You, my darling...only you!"

I tell him..."What is it you want that I have not given you already...If I have not given you everything...If you feel I have held back which I have not...then please know, I surrender...take me...I am yours.

Your body is not a battlefield and you do not have to surrender my dear
anyplace, anywhere, anytime I will find your erotic frontier

With me you will breathe loudly and uncontrollably by my touch
your body will crave for more, it will quiver of pleasure ready to be released so much

Out of control you do not surrender, but affectionate you will give in
slowly your body takes over by my command – and you give in to sin

And at that moment I whisper – I am going to take you
In the explosion I ram you – and you disappear into a zone of massive satisfaction - you

Waited

Monica

As he comes up to me from behind...all day I have ached for him...I waited.

I love it when he holds me...I am safe.

As he stands behind me...I know I do not have anything to fear...I see through his eyes and long for that cosmic journey we will soon be taking...I waited for this.

As he stands behind me, I know I am loved...I will go anywhere with him...take me there...because I waited my whole life for this.

As he stands behind me...I am his...undress me...I am yours...I waited for your hands to not only undress my body, but to undress my soul.

As he stands behind me...I wait to be taken as I know he will...I waited to feel his essence grow with excitement.

My beloved...take me...I waited all day for you...for your touch and your touch alone.

Captivated

I stand behind her – the fragrance mesmerizes my mind

Captivated

I gently touch her body and caress her soul as I stand behind

Captivated

I lean against her – she cannot escape the spartan

Captivated

I grow into her waiting secret garden while it hardens

Anytime

Monica

He comes up to me…I slowly back up…only the wall braces me.
His hand slowly moves my hair to the side…his arms spread my arms above my head.
His body so close to mine, I feel every inch of him…the weight of his body sends me in a dizzying dance.

Who is breathing for who…I feel as I am breathing through him.

His lips eager to find that spot…he knows it well…he knows what happens when even his breath reaches that place.
He knows I melt…before his lips even touch me.

I tremble…I shake…I can barely whisper…" Yes…yesssss"

After that pleasure ride, he lies there besides me
he is looking in my eyes with a gentle smile
I´m relaxed and satisfied, and yet I want more of him, his soul to see
my heart needs more of that body and mind – feeling juvenile

I gently touch his chest, and slowly move my fingers downwards to seek
he responds with pride – leans over me and whispers – are you naughty Miss Lee
Short of breath I whisper back – maybe – he answers, okay I will take you were you want to be
Caressing all my sweet spots, he once again takes me to a cosmic joy and peak

It is like he knows me – speaks through me

I´m Scared

Monica

I know these are my words to you...and right now...my words are "I'm scared".
With everything going on in the world...I am scared.
Right now, I am scared that I will not be able to hold you...see you...feel you.... touch you.

My heart is so heavy...I finally find the love of my life...the one that my heart was created to love.
You, my beloved, are the only one that has ever been able to calm my storms...right now, I need you...I am scared.
This ache in my heart.... I just wish I could reach out and caress your face...just to feel your breath on my fingertips would quiet my spirit.... because right now, I am scared.
My heart is racing, the tears flow from my eyes, my stomach feels like millions of angry butterflies are trying to fight inside...I am scared.

I am usually the brave girl that is strong for everyone else...but my darling...right now, I cannot breathe...I...am...just...scared....

Darling - you are not scared
expressing your emotions just shows you are dared
The scaredness is merely an expression for love and freedom
that you dare express your sincere observations show that you fight the demon

You are not scared that you won't see me
you confuse your longing with anxiety
We already set a date and place
and I promise you I won´t be late – we WILL embrace

Yes, the world is crazy and sometimes vicious
but with the right glasses the world is delicious

First shift

Monica

My darling...you sleep, I will take the first shift.
I will watch over you as you drift off into a realm of peace and relaxation.
Let sleep renew you...I will watch over you.

From where I am, I will guard you so that no bad dreams come to you.

I long for the day that I can finally be right next to you to have our nighttime ritual...where we walk through the house together....making sure things are put up and all the doors are locked, lights are out.

Darling we will crawl into bed I will lean against you while we read a bit as we wait for sleep to come to us.

As your eyes get heavy and you get comfortable on your side of the bed...I will be right there as I always imagined, pictured, envisioned.
I will be right there to watch over as you sleep just as I did from the 5,287 miles that we had between us in the beginning...just as I did on the first shift.

Jørgen

You have been taking shifts for everybody since you were little
It´s time to let go – no more shifts
it´s your time to be watched over, while you in your sleep are brittle
I will take over from here so you can relax when you drift

No more shifts

Sleep

Monica

My beloved......I cannot sleep...I cannot rest...I need to be by you.
I have waited my whole life to have sleep. I always said I was an eternal insomniac......my sleep was nonexistent. I paced for what seemed like thousands of miles every night...anxiously looking for something...someone.

I could never put my finger on it...what was calling me in the night to be so wide awake.
I truly believe it was my soul that was on alert...already preparing me for you. Through the miles...across the world...your soul called to mine.

Now...after 46 years...my soul found you....and now my thoughts of you take me to places of love and peace.
The restless nights...nights of no sleep will finally go away.
My soul will finally have rest as I lay in your arms....so safe...so secure...but most of all...so loved.

A deep sigh of relief as my heartbeat syncs with yours...as my breathing matches yours...another glance up at you...slow...slow...slower...until...sleep embraces us...good night my beloved.

Nica, sink into the deep

Nica, it´s the place where you can reap

Nica – now fall into sleep

Nica, I´m there to keep

Midnight and The Moon

Monica

Midnight....my favorite time of day.
The time of day when it is the darkest and yet my vision is the clearest.
Before I knew where you were...or even knew your name, I would walk outside every night at midnight and speak to the moon...she always listened to me speak about you.
I would tell her all the things I love about you.

While others laughed in disbelief that you existed, my friends, midnight and the moon always agreed with me.
I could picture us walking at midnight... barefoot... spring, summer, fall or winter... hand in hand and I point up at the moon and tell her..."Look, he is here...my Cosmic Supernova is here!"

Those visions are now a reality...because the moon loves me so much...she shined brightly over me so you could see me...and here we are!
I want the rest of my midnights for the rest of my life to be with you so we can walk hand in hand, and I can show the moon my beloved Midnight Runner.

Isn´t it beautiful how the Universe conspired to bring The Moon Goddess and The Midnight Runner together……what a beautiful coincidence.

Jørgen

Dear Moon Goddess

Midnight is your favorite time because you can feel free and open
the day captures you in so many binding ways which are broken
Luna is so bright; it resembles dreams of which love is woven

The fact that light is dark is an ever-challenging paradox
The fact that you have been so patient and waiting like the three bears with goldilocks
shows that hope and love is worth living for – now your Midnight runner is in your mailbox

Existence

Monica

It is not about being face to face...day in and day out.

It is about knowing you exist that makes my heart smile.

Jørgen

Existence

is about being soul to soul in co-existence

how else will you know you exist

Face to face is only grace when you are liberated

I do not exist; I do not have existence I ex-ist and I am ex-isting

Pictures of You

Monica

It is Sunday evening…I sit here and get myself together and prepare for the week…so much going on…so much to prepare for.

As I sit here at my desk, I glance over at your pictures.
Your smile is so bright and so full of life.
Your eyes have such soul and wisdom.
Your arms remind me that when I am scared, they will hold me and keep me safe.

When I look at your pictures…I see that you are my inspiration to be better each day. There are times that I just want to say, "I can't", but when I see you looking at me from the frame…I keep going.

You are my strength to get through each minute. Some days are just so hard, but when I look at your pictures, I see your smile and it gives me strength to be better than I was the minute before.

You are my moral compass when I want to say, "fuck it" and go off my track. When I look at your pictures, I see your eyes and they guide me back to my path, my journey.

You are my peace when the world is spinning out of control and I cannot get my balance. When I look at your pictures, I see your soul and I can feel it embrace mine to calm me down.

You are my protector.... when I am scared. When I look at your pictures, I see your arms and I know that is where I run to...where you will hold me and keep me safe.

You are my guide, that voice of serenity when I am restless. When I look at your pictures, I can hear your voice bringing me to a place of calm where I can melt into sleep as you watch over me.

I love these pictures of you....and...I love you.

The pictures you

- *paint of me is only reflected personality*
- *look at are merely an optimized resolution of reality*
- *hold so dear are so far the closest you have me near*
- *interpret and consume to keep away fear*
- *take in your soul, spirit, and mind*
- *see in my eyes and smile you will find*

To be true when you

- *Kiss my smile for the first time*
- *are being held in my arms and you feel everything is fine*
- *look in my eyes and realize, that they for you really shine*

Sundays

Monica

Sundays are for being lazy and laying next to you.

I can picture us on a Sunday getting up from being out the night before…what time is it? Who cares…because time means nothing to us on Sundays.

I can picture us on a Sunday laying in bed….my fingertips trace your trail to paradise as you smile in anticipation of where my hands will go.

I can picture us on a Sunday as my mouth reaches up to yours to kiss you and leave a trail from your neck to wherever I want to explore…..seeing your eyes watch me, gives me pleasure.

I can picture us on a Sunday with my legs wrapped around you pulling you in deeper…closer.

I can picture us on a Sunday looking up at you while you look down at me with my back arched.

I can picture us on a Sunday with storm clouds outside…. the thunder rumbles but not loud enough to cover my sounds of ecstasy.

I can picture us on a Sunday with our breathing fast and heavy like the rain outside.

I can picture us on a Sunday wide eyed and electric from the orgasmic vibrations we created and not just from the lightning flashing.

I can picture me on a Sunday laying next to you.... what time is it? Who cares...? Because time means nothing to us on Sundays.

Jørgen

You are right darling, on Sundays time means nothing in the sense of obligations
but it means everything in the meaning of co-existence, connection, and conversations

- and
on some days your back will arch so much while I´m in you and hold your breasts

La Petite Mort

Monica

La Petite Mort.... you are the owner, the creator of my orgasms.
It is only you that I want to explore with.... only you to touch my body to give me pleasure.
You are the one that breathes that orgasmic bliss into me.
The breath that I inhale from you...fuels that energy flowing into every cell of my body.... head thrown back lost, in that realm of passion and erotic escape.
You hold on to me, as I am so lost, dizzy with the pleasure you give.
Only looking at you to gather my composure so that you can do it all over again.... just with your breath...your touch....la petite mort.
But why is it called "the little death" when in that moment of pure orgasmic ecstasy I am more alive than ever before...all my senses heightened...it is not death you are taking me into...it is a rebirth of my sexuality with my Warrior...

Ma petite fille

"The little death" – I think, is an expression for the state where your soul takes you to a place where you are out of this world, and yet soooooo very alive

Orgasm is an empty spot waiting to be filled, that's why real sexy love is what we strive

Rich

Monica

You have made me the richest girl in the universe!
While others have their materialistic things in their lives to hold on to... I have you.
You are worth more than any material thing... you give me love so freely, so purely... truly... that is worth more than any amount of money, worth more than any mansion or car.
Nothing can compare to what I have with you.

Those that have it all... can sometimes be the poorest.

You have made me the richest because you give me the world... because you are my world!

If you replace the concept of being rich with the concept of gratefulness and humility
you will discover that the concepts of being poor or rich has no meaning
Their polarization is reversible, so they merely create invisibility
The state of gratefulness and humility is the most appealing

I´m truly humbled that I give you the feeling of being rich within the concepts of love and affection
It´s a liberating secure feeling where you feel the connection

Bareness

Monica

It is in that moment of bareness...when you connect body...mind and soul.
So vulnerable and so trusting of each other in that delicate space.
Nothing matters...just you...just him and in that space is where love leads the most beautiful love making you can imagine...raw...pure...passion.
I come up to meet you...up there somewhere.
When I rush to greet you...my soul is bared.

I am safe in his arms...he is safe in my arms...bare...

The one who is bare is brave and authentic
She who can bear bareness must also be demure
if you can bare yourself, you can walk through the obscure
you are the same – Idem – you are identic

The space of bareness is transparent for those who can transcend
You can be bare in my arms because our souls are immanent

When I meet you in the bareness – I will be bare
Intimacy becomes freedom released from our hearts – we give in to dare

My Muse

Monica

I remember going to the museum for the first time when I was a little girl.
The art on the walls was so beautiful that even as a young girl I was moved with emotions that I cried.

For me... when I see you, I am moved with emotions that I am in awe of you... I cry.
You are my muse... I want to write stories about you, yet I fear that words will do no justice to describe you.
I want to sing and dance to music that you create in me....my body just moves in a way that it has never moved before....this music is the most beautiful my ears have ever heard.
You bring forth creativity from a depth of my soul I did not know existed. Words that only you can create in me.

Ahhhh you are the delicious muse that erotic dreams are made of.

Stories written... even while I dream of you making love to me.... so powerful that I wake up in a delicious orgasmic state ready to pen what just happened even though my body still trembles.
Yes, my love...you are my muse... you are the words that ooze from my soul, the music my spirit dances to, the

energy in my bliss.... you are art that is too beautiful to hang on the walls of museums.
You are muse of poetry and stories.... you are the muse of memories I want to create with you, because of you.

You, my beloved, are the muse of our lives that we will create so magnificently.

Jørgen

Darling, I am so honored to be considered your muse
inspiration means "breathe in" and that is what you make me choose
breathe in your spirit and try walking in your shoes

Creation, dancing, writing, erotic dreams, and poetry
all qualities that are liberated to be released in symmetry

Home

Monica

I want to go home now. Home to where you are.

If you can be homesick for a place...you can also be homesick for a person...and I am.
Home is not just a house with 4 walls... home is where your heart is...and my heart is with yours.

I want to go home now... where we walk the streets hand in hand.
Home to make dinner for you and do laundry...so simple yet means so much to me.
Where we go grocery shopping and have friends and family over.

I want to go home now... where I can lay in bed next to you and there will be no more nightmares as you hold me.

I want to go home now where I can feel your love through your kiss, your touch, see it in your eyes.

I just want to go home now...

My dear

Your heart is already home - it knows

Even though it has not seen it – it can paint the hearts and the scenes

and with all that love to give the reality will expose

the beauty of reality as an art and what it means

I´m your home, I hold your heart, it´s no longer homeless

Read To Me

Monica

My darling…. when we had our "date night" and the topic of reading came up….my body reacted in a way that was quite erotic.
The mere thought of you wearing your glasses….and the sound of your voice as you hold a book reading to me.

I want to lay my head in your lap and look up at you while you read to me.
Leaning up against your chest while we are in bed…my fingers playing with the tufts of chest hair…. mmm mmm mmm.

The sight of seeing you in bed reading…..oh honey….makes me want to climb on top and have my way with you…get lost in the words that go from the page to your lips to my ears.
Promise me that you will always read to me…. that we will always share those erotic moments lost in words.

Jørgen

Of course I will read to you Miss Lee, while you lay in my lap and I caress and play with your hair
it´s just that I sense that there is so much more in the air

I will read to you the most interesting things, curious subjects and maybe some incitement
but again, I sense I also have to read something with excitement

While you are laying there in my lap, and I discover that you are no longer really listening
instead you are focused on my chest, and have that very endearing and alluring glance
I will slowly take off my glasses, and ask why you suddenly become glistening
You will just answer with a naughty smile, and I will teach you a lesson that takes you into trance

I will put you in the exact right position – lean over you and read/whisper some words in your ear
and I will slowly punish/pleasure you for being naughty, and you will beg me to be soooo near
It will be a punishment you won't regret, a pleasure you almost can't take
While holding you in a firm grip, your loins will press against mine, and there is no brake

You won't be able to control your body's search for pleasure, and you moan in sexual affection
the punishment slowly invades your body, and you explode in a cosmic orgasm, and feel the injection

Freedom

Monica

*Freedom... something so many take for granted.
Ahhhh but me... no, I embrace it because I am just now able to feel it.*

*The freedom to be me....to speak my mind even though I may not have the right answer....or my answers may be a 3000 word dissertation that takes you on a scenic route to get to my point that I was trying to make but had way too many metaphors and symbols in order to get my story out there but I know even in my run on sentences you let me be free to run on and on and on....you always sit there and let me ramble incessantly sometimes in my own funny way and sometimes in my emotional tear filled state and most of all my curious tell me more tell me more posture. (See...I did it again) ... you never judge me...
you just let me be free!*

*Even when Cs and Ws are mixed up...when I forget to put the "color" in my "color", I know you give me the freedom to say my silly thoughts and you will not judge me.
You give me the freedom to let my mind go in so many directions and expand with our conversations.*

I feel like I am floating in "free state" with you because you hold me up and let me dance with you…you are MY FREEDOM!
Never have I had the freedom to feel so raw and so vulnerable yet so safe and so secure.

Freedom feels so fucking good…so bare…perfectly naked where I truly feel like a goddess free to be who she is in her own skin……free….so fucking free!

Jørgen

Freedom as a phenomenon will always have borders
it´s the kind of borders that decide the feeling of freedom it orders
Could one have the liberty to feel free in being?
Could you take freedom and unchain it to freeing?

I love the thought about you feeling free
I love to watch you be
I´m able to see the effect of your freedom through love, happiness and immense energy
the urge to live your life at the fullest and in entropy

Self-Torture

Monica

Sometimes…the cruelest of self-torture…is to love somebody so much and not be able to express it enough for fear this lifetime will simply not show even one ounce.

Jørgen

True love is a gift for life, effete right there is no torture only devotion
Express, access, caress, and undress

Panduro

Monica

Panduro... such a wonderful name... a name to want... a name to have.

Jørgen

The syllable "Pan" means "everything" and the syllable "duro" means hard
I like to think of the name, as one to honor by having a broad perspective
The sense to comprehend everything, and therefore nothing on the chart
Transcend the mind in a reflective panopticon to get the essentials and be connective

In an audio/visual way it has both a good resonance and an aesthetic expression
One I have and cherish – one to give to the only who takes my heart with affection

Deep inside

Monica

Deep inside of my heart is where I hold you.

Deep inside of my soul is where you breathe.

Deep inside of my mind is where you challenge me...meet me...push me...encourage me.

Deep inside of me is where I want you, to feel every part of you...to see every bit of you.

Deep inside of me is where I want you...today, tomorrow and the day after that... forever... deep inside of me...

To be deep inside of you, I need to be deep inside of me
To be deep inside goes both ways, only love can let that light shine
Our souls have to, not only connect, but transcend each other you see

It seems I´m already there – present in your soul and mind
I know you´re searching through mine and that feeling is so kind

The spirit suddenly appears and asks – what is my existence at the empty spot between your souls?

Red Lipstick

Monica

Just so you know...

I was always told to never leave home without my red lipstick, always powder my nose and have just a touch of blush on... that is what proper girls do. Also, when wearing red lipstick it has to be a modest shade of red, just enough to give a slight color to your lips, because again, you are a "proper" girl and don't want to attract too much attention.

Well....

I went the total opposite direction...my red lipstick is vivid and bold. For me, red lipstick makes me feel sexy and sensual. It makes me feel wild, free and awakened. When I speak to you as I wear my red lipstick, it makes me think of all the places I want to see my red lipstick on you and all the conversations I want to have with you as well.

Red lipstick to speak words of love to you. So, you can not only see my red lips move, but you hear my words of passion and true love. The conversations we have no matter what they are about are deep like the color red that paints my lips.

As you leave for work in the morning my red lips would kiss yours so softly as we part for the day, such a gentle reminder as you see that ever so soft hint of red upon you that I am with you all day.
It is 3 pm I will welcome you home from your day at work and my red lips will brush yours as I hug you and move them to your neck. Again, another note of red upon your body as a reminder that I was there.

When we are out and about, I will wear my red lipstick. So, when I am not standing near you and you are across the room, our eyes will meet, and you will see me mouth the words... I love you!

Standing next to you, whispering in your ear...." Let's go home", leaving a touch of red on you once again....and not just your cheeks from you blushing with other words said after that.

As we get home and are behind our closed doors, my red lips begin to streak your body from top to bottom in a wild frenzy as if this is my greatest creation of body art on you. Nothing is untouched.... hues of red on every inch of you... the sweetest perfection!

Looking up at you, you see my now smeared red lips moaning and saying your name as waves of pleasure flow through me.

Spent afterwards and to the shower we go as the hot water washes the day of red lipstick off only for us to sleep so we can wake up and let a new day begin in the life of my red lipstick.

PS... I will always wear my red lipstick for you, darling.

Jørgen

I will kiss your lips anytime
red, blue, natural - I even pretend to kiss them in this rhyme

Your lips are wonderful, they are shaped like kindness and suggestion
painted in red – if I will kiss them? Don´t ask, it´s a rhetorical question

When you cover my body with your red lips
I will shiver under your gentle kiss

Wearing your color red
I guess everything is said

Let me kiss you

Prelude

Monica

Prelude of a kiss…that kiss that awakens a passion that lies in wait.
That kiss that fills your lungs with bliss…hanging on to each breath.
That kiss that fuels the ecstasy within your soul.

Yes…oh yes, the prelude to……the perfect kiss.

Jørgen

Prelude to a kiss
Seduction to a bliss
I will take you miss

Behind Closed doors

Monica

Behind closed doors with you in our own little world.
Where we laugh, cry, sigh, sing and I dance for you.

Behind closed doors where I can bare my soul to you in the safety of your arms and know that you will keep my heart safe from the world and I do the same for you.

Where we talk about our dreams and plans for the future.

Behind closed doors is where we explore each other, not just our bodies but our minds.
The books we will read, the theories we will discuss and conversations within conversations that will go on and on.

Where I slither on top of you and get lost in the rhythmic motions of my body moving to climax then flipped on a dime to feel the delicious weight of you pressing into me, once again lost in the throws of your love, legs trembling, no worries about how loud my pleasure sounds are or that we are writhing in unison.

Behind closed doors where I can finally sleep after 46 years of being enemies with insomnia. You, my warrior, defeated her for me and I will now have peace as I sleep next to you.

Behind closed doors where we live, and dream is where I want to be…forever.

Jørgen

Behind closed doors openness is essential
both our bodies and minds are confidential
It´s a refuge for bodily and mental extension
It´s where we have deep conversation and comprehension

With open doors we live off the closed doors
we stretch our consciousness with what we synthesized
Through imaginary doors we do our chores
It´s so vivid and energized

In The Dark

Monica

Some people are afraid of the dark, they can't see and lose themselves even though in the dark all other senses are heightened, magnified and things are so clearer.

I would love to be in the dark with you. Lost in all my other senses with each at their peak.

In the dark hearing your words and the different tones, octaves as you speak, whisper to me. Where are you? I can only be led by your words. Feel free to tease my ears, I am yours... trembling with excitement.

The scent of you would be quite intoxicating. I would be drunk on the essence of your soul, your breath sending orgasmic shivers down my spine. Inhaling every part of you.

In the dark I am under your spell.... feed me. The taste of skin, your lips, all of you sends me into a dizzy state.

Your touch like electricity sending pulses to every cell in my body. Awakening every part of me. Breathless with the anticipation of where you will touch me next as you explore.

In the dark I see you so clearly as if the lights were on. I see my darling and his beautiful blue eyes that at first sight hypnotized me. I see his smile that is so full of vibrant energy. I see my warrior so full of life and love that each moment that goes by, I fall more and more in love with him if that is even possible.
If only people would not be afraid of the dark, they would find pleasure beyond the measure of what is in front of them.

So, my love, I must say, thank you for diving into the darkness with me. I promise when it is your turn, you will be very aware of how intense your sight will be....in the dark.... let us go!

Jørgen

My darling – the light is black, but we don´t see
that the beauty of the dark is in the light where we feel free
The darkness has a different echo and influence
Senses are alert in a continuance

When you enjoy the darkness, I understand
it´s the small amount of light that constitutes the dark
It´s the place and state that takes us to heartland
come take my hand into the light black without remark

Voice of The Silent Warrior

Monica

Every goddess needs her warrior.

That is what you are for me... my warrior.

When I am scared, I can feel the presence of my silent warrior as he stands guard behind me protecting me, and his words echo in my soul...I got you.

When I am happy and it is a good day, I can see the joy in his eyes and no words are needed from my silent warrior...his eyes so bright speak louder than any words.

As I sleep my silent warrior hovers over me to make sure I am resting and if nightmares come to me, he fights them off before they enter my dream realm.

My silent warrior has taken all the pieces of my heart and with his powerful love he has put them all back together and made me whole again.

His love is louder than the voices of the millions of souls around me... he is my beloved, my protector, he is....my silent warrior.

When you reach the point where silence is a strength
where your glance substitutes your words with affinity
Where the smile of your soul reveals the length
of what has become a love with infinity

Hush hush - the silence is sounding in the air
my eyes will caress your soul with care

Dressed In Love

Monica

Most women think about every little detail of their outfit that they wear, the perfect shoes, must always have the perfect outfit not to mention those huge statement pieces of jewelry. Oh...and let's not forget the makeup and the hair that must be on point. Flawless and exactly right!

But my love, since I have been with you, people no longer notice the clothes I wear, how my hair looks or my makeup...not even my shoes or my jewelry.

No, what they notice is the smile on my face instead of my lipstick, my eyes that sparkle instead of my mascara and eye shadow, my cheeks flushed instead of blushed. They see that my skin glows and radiates as I ooze love for you. They notice my feet that have more life and energy in them instead of my shoes. They notice everything that you make me feel on the inside that flows to the outside.

I have been told this numerous times that they can see that I am a woman in love. Even when you tell me I look beautiful, my response to you is "What you see is a reflection of my love for you."

A close friend of mine told me not that long ago..." Monica Lee you wear love well." I responded to her and said...." I am dressed in love...the outfit that he so lovingly dresses me in daily"

Even if I were to walk outside completely naked, people would not notice.... they would only see that I am completely dressed in your love.

Jørgen

The dress of love I have given you costs nothing
yet it is the most precious gift I can give you
It has no size or special cut, and even though it makes you blush
of love in mesmerizing radiation that I can see through

In love you are all dressed up and everywhere to go
With your glow you have everything to show

My love suits you because of your soul and appearance
"I love you" is my dress, shoes, jewelry, and makeup to your grace
You deserve this because of your adherence
When I see you dressed in my love – I want to embrace

Part 2

Meaningful conversations

Prelude

Picture it, the bright sun shining on his face from the window as he sits at his dining room table. Me at my desk with my hair, makeup, and jewelry on and dressed for my phone date with him. His eyes changing colors as the light fades from afternoon to evening then to night. I watch his every move, his every gesture as I am still in awe of this beautiful creature in front of me on the screen. I stare at him intently from time to time just getting lost in him. He stops speaking to ask me "What, Nica?" (his nickname for me is Nica which is short for Monica). I reply to him and say..." I am just taking you in". His face flushes and a bright smile flashes. Even his eyes shine brilliantly as his lips curve into a bashful smile. The music playing in the background, and the conversation continues.

Thousands of hours we have spent in conversation sometimes so deep it is hard to come back from and other times we laugh until our faces hurt. No one conversation has been the same. There have been quiet moments we share even as we face each other through the screens, but all I can do is imagine myself actually sitting across from him to give me some peace as one day that I know that is how it will be.

My dream is to be there to reach out and touch his hand as we speak. My fantasy is to get up from my seat in the middle of a conversation and kiss him as he is lost in his train of thought.

Introduction

Have you ever just had a conversation that blew your mind, and you were left spent afterwards in this sapiosexual orgasmic glow with your legs quivering? If you haven't then, you are missing out. The conversations that Jørgen and I have, are intense, passionate, intriguing, comical and refreshing. It is like making love and when it is over, I am left in an afterglow of pure orgasmic conversational bliss!

Why do I compare our conversations to making love? To set the record straight, our conversations are not always sexual in nature, but I am comparing it to something so beautiful such as making love. When we speak, he flips the conversation into different positions, taking it slow then gradually to a more deeply intense level. He is in control of the subject and I ride the words he gives me no matter what topic we are speaking about where I am excited and squirming in my seat wanting to hear more from him. Somewhere in the conversation, I take over and my words are surrounding him, seducing his mind, his spirit as we become more excited about what we are speaking about until we get to a climax of thoughts, concepts and beliefs in which we fall into ecstasy and he draws me in closer for that post conversation orgasmic glow.

We all crave to be heard. We all want to dive deep into conversation and whether it may be way over our heads or is a conversation within a conversation. Sometimes people can be shy at first or maybe they are just not "big talkers". Maybe they are just shut down and can't open up because of various reasons. But when you are in a new relationship you must have crucial and meaningful conversations to know if either of you are on the same page.

We are still in the middle of a global pandemic and I still cannot get to him or him to me. Our weekend dates are still happening the best we can from screen to screen. It is through these times that we have, that he has given me intimacy in such a way that most people don't understand when they are face to face. So many people think that intimacy must be physical....it isn't. Intimacy of conversation, mental foreplay if you will, is quite erotic. What is intimacy of conversation? It is that closeness you gain through being raw, vulnerable, honest, open, scared, and peaceful. Emotional intimacy comes in to play as well and should be one of the top things that occurs with couples. Being able to share those emotional times is like glue for the relationship that creates a deep bond in the union....and yet so many skip this part and go straight for the sex, the fun times. When this happens and the hard times come up it is very trying. Hard times are difficult enough but when you are not sure how to speak to the other person or you are not sure if you are on the same page it makes things harder and can eventually cause such a riff that there is a break up.

What you are about to read in Part 2 "Meaningful Conversations" are actual conversations that we have had. We feel that these are 8 crucial conversations that every couple should talk about and work on throughout each phase of a relationship. There may be other conversations that are also important to be had, but these are ones we chose to speak about. These concepts can change in how you feel in different times of your relationship, but for us just starting out this is what you are going to see. I cried a lot, as it forced me to totally come out of the dark. In Part 1 you saw me pour my soul out in such a way that I felt like if I didn't, I would internally combust. Now, what you are going to see is a transcended step in our relationship.

I just love sitting across from him even if it is on the other side of the screen and hearing his ideas, thoughts, and words. I may not be physically in front of him, but I can feel him holding me, keeping me safe when I speak. This is something I am not used to, but have felt so at peace that I melt right into him.

Part 2 is about being able to truly let yourself speak from your heart on hard topics. If you can talk about these concepts, you can gauge where you and your partner stand. Are you on the same side of the topic or are you both so different from each other that you may have to step back and take inventory of your emotions? Or here is the best part.... are you able to see things from another point of view and have an open mind when you hear what your partner has to say? When Jørgen and I started this journey in writing this book we wanted to give hope and inspiration to others not just because we are in a long distance relationship, but because we wanted to share how conversation and speaking your soul can be liberating and is the foundation to keep the union solid.

From Poetic Longing to Meaningful Conversations - Monica

Being

Awareness on being
is being aware

Jørgen

Monica

Hi, my name is Monica Lee. Some people call me Mona, Mona Lisa, Mon, Moni, Batgirl, but my beloved calls me "Nica". I love that name. I introduce myself because I want to introduce you to my "being". I actually have my practice set up as "The Sensual Art of Being", more on that later. I am 5ft 2 and 3/4 inches of passion, fire, intensity, sensuality, love, culture, emotions, laughter, love, silliness, seriousness, ambition, drive, sex and did I mention, love.

I am a Sex Educator, Relationship/Intimacy Coach, Writer, Blogger, Motivational Speaker, Personal Cheerleader at your service (you're welcome), Lover of Life, Connoisseur of the Virgin Adult Beverages (especially my favorite Long Island Ice Tea minus the Long Island), Moon Goddess (yes, my favorite time of day is midnight so I can go dance, bare under the moonlight), Certified Tantra Educator/Practitioner, Wannabe Comedian, A Seeker, A Lover, A Storyteller (weaver of adult bedtime stories...dreams), Full Time Student of The Universe (always learning from those around me), and Radio Show Host of Front Porch Sex Talk with Monica Lee.....whewwwww that was a mouth full!!

This is me... all of me, with a touch of dramatics at times, but for the most part this is me. Mother, sister, daughter, friend, bestie, comadre, tia, girlfriend and lover.

I talk too much, think too much, and give you the scenic route in a conversation that goes on and on while I try to get my point across. I try not to be a reactor when I am listening or watching others. Instead I try to listen, watch, and process. I believe this is what hurts people the most - is that they listen to react. They do not listen to process. In those brief moments we can help or hurt someone by reacting and not processing. I am scared at times and retreat in those moments to reflect and lick my wounds. It is hard for me to reach out for help because I am a doer, a giver. I am vulnerable and just now able to start showing that side of myself to Jørgen.

"Being" is defined by some as our essence, our existence in this world, but upon the view of who? Who decides who we should be or what we should be? When I speak of "to be" I am speaking in the context of "being". The moment we are born we are conditioned to "be" who others think we should "be". We are conditioned on what others think love is, how we should view sex and sexuality, race, acceptance and how we look just to name a few. The list goes on and on. We are even conditioned on how to be in relationships and marriage. So, to find your soul mate in

a world that is completely different from what you are used to or what you are conditioned to know can be quite daunting.

We must step back and let go of the guilt, shame, condemnation, and other pre-existing conditions that have been engrained into us. We have to go back to that moment of birth and wipe our slates clean and form our own "being". This can be difficult for some as it totally goes beyond family relationships and what the "norm" is within that familial structure. For some it can be a traumatic experience to let go of those things we know so that we can have a chance at life with a new vision. For some it means that the family turns their back on them because they are an embarrassment or a shame to their family. For some it can even mean liberation when they decide to break free to live their true authentic self and find out who they really are without the smoke screens and mirrors.

So many people go through life not knowing who they are or what they are... or understand their being. It is a life of complacency and just living as a spectator on the sidelines of their own life. We do what we are told and follow the rules, not that we should be breaking the rules, but sometimes we have to in some instances. I saw a movie one time where the youngest daughter was not allowed to get married because she was the one that was supposed to stay behind and take care of the mother as she grew older. Her life was going to be that of servitude. Even though she fell in love and knew this man was her soul mate, she was forbidden and cursed to not marry him. Can you imagine living a life of pain, suffering and utter heart break because you could not have your beloved? Can you imagine not being able to be your true self because you were told that your life, your existence is to be what somebody else dictates? I call these generational curses that must be broken. These are the conditions that we have placed upon us before we are even born into existence. We don't stand a chance at life or Being until we break free of that. Some hold those traditions and conditions in reverence and follow their life in such a way. I guess I am too much a of a rebel goddess and want to help others find their place in this world.

In relationships we follow the normal flow of things or what we consider normal. We exist, we grow up to date the good boy or good girl, they have to be in our circumference in area so that we do not move away, we have children, and we die. Kind of sums it all up, right? But what if you find yourself in relationship after relationship because everybody in your so-called circumference is not who you vibe with? I have seen so many people say "Monica, this is not working for me. I am doomed to be alone forever". I know those words all too well. In relationships we are taught to not show our suffering, we are taught to be quiet and not show who you really are because honey, if they knew your family was bat shit crazy they would run for the hills. We are taught as women to look a certain way, be a certain way, act a certain way. Some of these things are just impossible, because of so many factors outside our control. I would love to be a perfect little porcelain china doll; however, genetics proves that to be difficult. Sadly, some people even base their view of being on just what is around them. When you break down those barriers and thought processes of what your "type of person" is, throw out the fucking map of where they should live in comparison to you, step outside your box of comfort and what you were taught to be, you might just find love out there in this great big world.

Do not let society dictate your life.... damn. We are human beings put on this earth to help other humans to "be". As parents we teach our kids the rights from wrongs and should give them the freedom to discover their true existence. We should never put limits or boundaries on them. If we do that, then we snuff out the reason why they are here, hence causing a ripple effect of void for others. We should always have the right to determine what we do, feel, live, have, or not have. How beautiful is it to live a life to just… be free to explore all the wonderful things we can think of.

I love what I do because I help many people take that eraser and wipe away all those conditions of their Being and give them a new start at life, love, and happiness. One of the saddest things I have seen in my career is the woman who is non orgasmic because she was told that women are not sexual. A woman is to be with her husband, notice I said husband, and let him have his pleasure. She is taught that sex is for procreation and her husband's pleasure. Her sexuality, her essence, her love, her being, her Divine Goddess means nothing. She goes a lifetime of not having pleasure, not having that sexual energy course through her veins to be channeled in her life. She goes a lifetime to just be a bystander in her own life… not feeling, not thinking, just existing without her true essence. When I work with women like this and tell them to give themselves permission to wipe the slate clean it is as if a butterfly comes out of her cocoon. Her true Being bursts out to finally breathe.

When I see men and women held back from a life of beautiful existence, I want to run up to them and shake them into an awakened state. Men go through this as well. They are conditioned to be a certain way, or they are not "manly" enough. To be a true man is to love and show his vulnerability as a strength, not as a weakness.

The art of sensual being is to be your true authentic self. To go against the grain of what we are taught from birth and how we are to perceive things. We are conditioned certain ways within our cultures. We are born a clean slate. The artsy goddess I am always loves to use the canvas as an example. Keep your slate clean and as you navigate through life, create your own museum of masterpieces. Live your divine life and be the badass warrior spreading badassery throughout the land. Be the Divine Goddess.

With all of this said, I am a goddess in all my sensual being. I let it ooze it from my soul. When I walk, my hips sashay. When I speak, my words are slow and my voice is a tone that many compliment, but not only do my lips say the words, but my eyes do as well. My soul will always embrace you and let you feel love. I always wear tube tops in the summer and sometimes my makeup is on point and sometimes I am au' naturale. I love everybody and give too much before I give to myself. I am a free thinker and never judge. Occasionally, I stumble and forget that I have come so far in my journey. I have risen from the ashes and at times I have sat in those dark clouds with the plumes surrounding me and choked. But every time, I rise stronger than ever to be... me. I wiped my slate clean a long time ago, let go of curses that held me back and awakened my goddess. When I did that, I never turned back. Some people in my life stayed where they were as it was not fitting for them to see someone like me in their life. It was against what they felt was right for them. I never hesitate to move on, and I teach others to keep moving as well on their path because life is short and precious. Not everybody will be on your side and won't understand your beautiful Being. That is ok because someone out there will see it, want it, vibe with it, embrace it and love it.

This is me....

Jørgen

I am astonished about the way Monica can write and pinpoint the essence of being in an everyday context. It is so spot on, honest and straight from the heart – I love it.

I have a slightly different way to describe it, in comparison to what Monica wrote.

Of all concepts you could argue that "to be" or "being" is the substance or predominantly basic character of the human being, therefore the carrier of all other

concepts and how they are expressed. By that, I mean that the core of the being you possess and carry is what emerges from you and determines how all other concepts are being presented or displayed.
If we take a look at the concept "being" it has been a subject for discussion in philosophy since Aristotle and forward to this day with different meanings, discourses and different contexts. Aristotle is considered the father of ontology, meaning the teachings of the beings. The beings are a complex concept, as you can discuss it and philosophize about it in different areas, aspects, and appearances. However, there is no truth, consensus, or valid conclusion of what "being" is or what it consists of. In the present text I will direct my attention on "being" as being present in the context of a human and how it as a phenomenon appears towards other beings and relationships.

If we go back to my assertion that the being is the substance of all other concepts and how those concepts are being displayed or appear, I want you to think of yourself as a being with no kind of character, no concepts. In fact, consider yourself as nothing but the being as you were born into before your brain had a consciousness, and was infected by specific character properties. I know this is difficult, because how do you do that? The German philosopher Edmund Husserl uses a term called "epoché".

He states that to perform an epoché, we must ignore all prejudices and theoretical knowledge, put it in brackets and step out of or transcend the natural attitude and perception we have. In this context he ignores his own and the outside world's consciousness and finds that it always is conscious about something that it is intentional and aimed at something. The problem with ignoring the consciousness is that it is the only quality we have to perform the epoché.

To perform an epoché is not easy and is paradoxical as you may have discovered. Some exercises that might help could be yoga, meditation, listening to specific music that calms you down to help you feel good, strip yourself for thoughts, or go meta in your mind. By looking at yourself as a being you view from the outside or above – either way your consciousness is working. The exercises are merely examples as there might be other methods. No matter how you get there, it will be a journey of learning and a healthy exercise for your consciousness, mind, and soul. If you can perform the epoché, you will be able to see yourself as a naked being ready to take on concepts and perform them in a new way.

To be able to see what it means in practice, you could try to notice how you, for instance, perform these concepts - love, trust, affection, respect, humility, sorrow, patience, and authenticity. These concepts are just examples, however, there could be other concepts you could use as well. How do you perform these concepts towards other beings and relationships? Is there anything you want to change? Are there areas or expressive ways where you use negative concepts? Could you listen more intensely before arguing? Could you show more patience? One thing you can´t do is to blame others for your behavior and use them as an excuse not to change. In this instance it can show that you haven´t understood the epoché or practiced it, and you still have the choice no matter of other beings.

Remember that Edmund Husserl said that our consciousness is intentional. That means that you might deceive yourself if you find excuses for performing a given concept in a good way or replace it with a bad concept. For example, if you use love disguised as manipulation or being constructive versus being abusive as well as other negative aspects. You must use your intention in a positive way to be a good being for other beings and relationships. Even though they might not have the same ability. If not, you could be constructive, listen and work with them. This will allow them to learn or dissolve the relationship as you can´t get through to let them know the reason why. To understand the intentions, reasons, or motives for a behavior, you will gain a better platform to act from and find an appropriate way to take further steps to a development of the relationship.

In any kind of relationship that is where you should start, by recalibrating through practicing the epoché. Everybody can change for something better, and the cliché "no one is perfect" has some meaning here. In fact, striving to be a better person throughout your life should be a main goal to succeed at being a good father, mother, sister, brother, man, wife, friend, colleague... etc.

For me to perform the epoché I use music that penetrates my soul and takes me to a melancholic yet constructive state of mind. I also go meta and look at myself and my actions toward other beings and relationships. I literally picture situations, look at myself from above or outside, and reflect on what I see.
By doing those epoché exercises my consciousness that sees and reflects on my conscious creates new consciousness and intentions.

Some of the features I have improved by performing epoché exercises are becoming a better listener by listening more intensely and being able to listen to the conversation within the conversation.
I also discovered that in some parts of my life I tended to be a little egotistical but did not know about it until I performed epoché exercises.

I also learned to be able to show and express my feelings more than I used to as I had a hard time opening. I also investigated different concepts I found interesting by looking into their etymology, to find out where they originated from, if they have several meanings, and to see different philosopher´s interpretations of them. A concept can suddenly appear in a new context with more than one perception which can lead to a new perspective of the concept.

So, by being curious about the world, your existence, your consciousness and by investigating concepts, you will be able to change in a positive way.

Communication

Give it to me hard, give it to me soft…raw, pure, open, and honestly!

Monica

Communication

Monica

Communication is always a key element in any relationship especially when you are thousands of miles away. How do you date and get to know one another when you are not only on different continents but different time zones?

In the beginning communication needs to be one of the most important things as you get to know each other. Let's face it, if you are not on the same page how are you going to evolve? It just can't be about sex. If we rely only on sex in the beginning, what happens when you open your mouth to speak? What happens when you really don't know what is going on in this connection? What happens when you have one view on love and the other person has a totally opposite view than you?

Conversation is becoming a lost art, and these days everybody is so preoccupied with a simple text or direct message typically abbreviated and not in complete sentences. It seems like communication is lost out there as there is a hook up culture that is all the rage no matter how old you are. Of course, that does not apply to everyone as there are people out there that are truly wanting to find love and relationships that are not all based upon sex with no conversation. They are wanting to get to know that other person.

People are drawn by the sex appeal, the visual which leads to the physical part. Yes, sometimes it can be good to just have that raw animalistic attraction, but again, what happens when you start to voice opinions, or want to talk about the future?

Let's kick it up a notch, when you are not on the same time zone or the same continent, not only do the miles separate you, but seven hours as well. For us, our conversations are all we have at the moment. I remember in the beginning my brain would hurt in a good way after spending 7, 8, 9 hours on face time with him. Saturdays around noon he would call me which was 7pm his time and we would just talk about such intense things that my mind was totally blown. I had always wanted to have those conversations with someone. Someone that would expand my knowledge, give me information that would feed my soul and challenge me. I was and still am addicted to our conversations we have; they are truly poetic. Almost as if they are a great symphony if you will. Starting out so beautiful like an adagio and flowing to move you. The questions, the responses intensifying into a powerful crescendo of words back and forth so powerful and profound that you are moved to tears, laughter, anger at times because of the subject. Every emotion you can think of has poured from our souls in our conversation, and finally into a decrescendo of softness, clarity, peace and love. He was and still is so attentive and as a true warrior he holds space for me while I speak.

I remember after one of the first few conversations we had, it was like a total outer body experience and he told me that through our conversations I was pulling him in closer. I cried because he was doing the same. I was already in love with him, but he realized he was falling for me at that moment (see, I joke with him and tell him he loved me but just didn't know it). It was total mental foreplay. Conversations about anything and everything and nothing, but like a beautiful symphony every time.

It is through such conversations that a couple can evolve without letting the physical dominate the relationship. The sex will ultimately come naturally. For most sapiosexuals it is through the conversations we have that... get my "biscuit buttered". Sex is wonderful and amazing, but once again, there are just a few miles between us and a nasty global virus holding us hostage at the moment.

Have fun and don't lose sight of your communication with each other as that can be so very intimate in nature with any subject. Whether you have been together 5 minutes or 50 years, keep those conversations going and guess what - sitting in complete silence is a beautiful conversation of energy being exchanged. Silence is just as powerful as words are.

Jørgen

Many relationships suffer and have devastating outcomes due to conversations that can turn into harsh discussions, shouting and emotional violence. One reason that this can happen is because the attention on the conversation is lost in accusations and fighting in order to protect your arguments, and come across with your own perspective.
If the attention in a conversation is directed towards meaningful listening, you might discover more than words coming out of the other person's mouth, and thereby find and see things in a broader perspective, - because after all – what is actually being said, and why?

Meaningful listening is crucial in any relationship. Often times the opposite is the reason to bad communication and misunderstanding which can lead to unhealthy being and presence.
When I use the term meaningful listening and not only properly, intense or genuine listening etc... it's because the

concept of being meaningful reveals that your presence and the fact that the person you are listening to perceives you as intersubjective and trustworthy. Besides that, you must also have an attention which the person feels is directed to her/him, so that the person feels that there is security within a relaxed atmosphere and can trust. That is meaningful to the person, and if listening isn't portrayed as such then it has no impact, and it has no sense.

To be able to listen in a meaningful way implies that you can create confidence and trust to the person you're listening to. When you have obtained and earned the confidence and trust, the next ability is to practice a multifaceted attention which means that you listen with more than one dimension and those dimensions are:

Listening to the –

- *verbal conversation –*
- *conversation within the conversation*
- *emotions, feelings, soul, and spirit – the being*
- *body-language*

These four dimensions characterize the meaningful listener. However, it's not an easy task. It requires a lot of practice and knowledge, but it is very essential not to mention valuable because of the effect and impact is has for the person, that you are listening to.

Here are some guidelines to use in a conversation for listening skills

- *You must let go of your own opinion while you are listening, otherwise you do not listen. Being able to do that creates the possibility to let the person be what she/he can be. If at the same time you are listening, are concentrating on your own opinion and defense, then you do not give the person a fair chance, because you miss what actually is being said.*
- *You must acknowledge the conversation and let it happen with energy that is in it. Remember that the person's existence is untouchable, but its values, opinions, and actions are exposed to criticism.*
- *The ability to sense the dramaturgy of the conversation – when is enough, enough?*
- *In Protreptic there is a Greek term called "Prosoché" that has 5 types of awareness that can be useful when you are practicing meaningful listening:*

    1. *To be aware of oneself*
    2. *To be aware of the other/others*
    3. *To be aware of what happens in the conversation/event*
    4. *To dare to attract attention*
    5. *To be aware of your own awareness*

To be a meaningful listener takes a lot of practice, but it is essential as I have learned over years. When you do master it, you will see a totally different world. As a result, the perspective of the subject discussed is broadened, which gives the conversation a lift. It could mean there are more openings, directions, a better understanding that challenges your own interpretations, prejudices and opinions.

If you just think of the above advice while having a conversation, you have come a long way.

To be a meaningful listener only requires your full attention and awareness.

If I had not listened meaningfully to Monica the first time we spoke, I would not have been able to respond to her version of the poem Crimson Tears with mine.

Freedom

Freedom is conditioned by the perception of limitation in infinity

Jørgen

Freedom

Monica

Where do I even start? Well, let me start by saying, I am a free spirit and I do free spirit shit! There, I got that off my chest. There was a time when I couldn't say that. Not everybody is afforded that luxury. It is sometimes ourselves that holds us hostage.

There are so many different aspects when we think of "Freedom". Freedom of speech, freedom to love who we want, freedom to live how we want to live, you get the picture. I want to focus on freedom in a relationship and freedom to "just be" which goes together.

When we think of freedom, we often think of doing what we want to do when we want to do it. Yes, true. Others may see freedom differently. Freedom to be your true authentic self is huge. If you don't have that, then you tend to lose yourself which can take a harsh turn in a relationship, cause you to doubt yourself and your existence within the union. You start to feel suffocated, trapped, unheard.

When freedom is absent in a relationship all sorts of negative flows in. For example, when we do not have the freedom to speak openly about what we feel, want, need, crave, or desire, then, that can open the door for others to listen. What may start out innocently as a "venting" session to someone else can potentially grow into something more. If we do not give our partner the freedom to speak of those things, we stifle their spirit and blow out their fire. Freedom is a fuel to fire our spirits to live our true life.

I have seen so many couples where one person is not able to speak freely because of being judged and condemned, which brings out the shame and guilt. It could be about anything, but one of the biggest issues brought to me to help with, is freedom of sexuality. Not every couple is equally matched in the sex drive department. However, if you do not allow your partner to speak freely about what they feel, need or even desire and you just judge them, that can potentially be harmful. Freedom can go both ways in this instance. If one doesn't have the freedom to be open about what they feel or want, and the other doesn't have the freedom to say why they feel negative towards that, it just becomes one big cluster fuck! This ties into the vulnerability and communication aspect. I work with couples where the wife wants to be free to be creative in their relationship, she needs to talk about her feelings and express her fantasies even if they are not acted upon. Yet the husband doesn't want to hear it, he just shuts her down. Her goddess within is put to sleep on a shelf. She feels lost and unheard. I used to be that person as well, shut down and shamed for what I am, what I do and how I feel. I lost my goddess, my divine feminine. I gained weight, I got sick... I was so lost and nowhere to turn.

It was one of the darkest times of my life. I was not able to express the sensual side of me. I was not able to release that sexual energy that fired me up and it ran cold in my veins. When I speak about sexual energy, I am talking about the life force we have within us. I use it to channel all my creativity and in all aspects of my life. When I work with couples, I help them awaken this life force to connect once again with each other. I not only work with couples, but with individuals who have never felt this or once did and got lost on the path. Once this energy is activated it is a conduit of open communication and a deep, blissful connection.

When the freedom is gone, and you cannot be your true self, it can lead to all kinds of downfalls. For me, it makes me physically ill. In my single life I gave myself permission to be free to heal, to express myself in all aspects of my life. I was finally able to be me. I was not going to let someone into my life after all my hard work and finally awakening my goddess again for them to take that away from me. I dated a man that took that freedom away from me to do what I do and be what I am. There was shame, guilt that flooded me and he was embarrassed to be with me. For a split second I thought about putting the goddess to sleep again and remembered how miserable I was, so that was a huge hell to the no! I passed the pop quiz The Universe gave me and after a few dates, it was over.

Fast forward to April 4, 2020 and here is Jørgen, this beautiful soul that understands freedom and encourages it. In this time of our long-distance relationship, it is so important for us both to encourage that in each other. All that he gives me, I give back to him. I love to watch him smile as I talk on and on. I am free to speak my mind and throw my ideas at him and he cheers me on. I am able to be what I am and do what I do, and he encourages it.

Not many people can understand what I do. For those I dated or those that tried to get to know me, they strongly said, 'No", I will not have my girlfriend talk about sex or help others. It can be quite challenging to be with someone like me because of that and seriously takes a strong and secure soul to do so. I cannot take their freedom away to feel as they do, and they cannot take away my freedom to do what I do. We have to love in such a way that we trust each other, respect is a given, but we have to respect the other person and let them dance to the music they hear. You may not be able to hear it, but they do, so let them be. Instead of condemning them for something you do not understand or can't see, let them be a free spirit. You can't cage a free spirit... they will wither and die.

It is an amazing feeling to love someone so much that they feel they are free and able to thrive. Jørgen has given me so much in such a short time. He has given me unconditional love, and immeasurable peace to heal my body. He has allowed me to grow into my vulnerability and gives me strength and courage, he has filled my emptiness, he fights my fears and calms my spirit. True intimacy that I craved and ached for he gives to me on a cosmic level. He is patient with me in my stressful and sometimes chaotic work schedules and within that he makes sure that I stay balanced and grounded. He listens with his heart, his mind and soul at my sometimes, incessant ramblings and gives me truth that I need to hear. But most of all, he gives me space for me to have freedom and just be... me.

I will never forget the words he said to me..." Freedom dances with beauty" ...I have said it already and I will say it again, over, and over... He is my freedom... my beautiful freedom!

If I can be Monica's freedom, it means that she is able to relax and find her own freedom because she doesn't have to fear anything, and with time we will find that both our freedoms are transcended into one entity.

To be able to write about freedom, could imply that I am a free spirit, and live a life were freedom is considered a civil right, within laws constituted by the society I live in. The fact is that there are laws, moral and ethics codes, norms and discourses that actually function as a limitation of freedom, a limitation of which there is a general agreement upon, by most of the society.

We have to remember that freedom is not a given thing. Wanting it, thinking or writing about it, can in some societies mean punishment, persecution or even death. This is usually due to religious beliefs, dictatorship, or undeveloped tribe beliefs.
As human beings our freedom is limited and yet at the same time, we can create freedom. Nature alone is a limit, and the examples of that is natural disasters like hurricanes, floods, earthquakes, and right now a virus (Covid-19), which has forced the world population to make restrictions that has a vast impact on the freedom we are used to.
But we are also capable of creating the future by our

actions, and thereby implicitly paint our freedom as we like it to be, which is within the given limitations, by which we have learned to live with.
It may be difficult to define the concept of freedom, because it depends on the point of view. One could argue that "it's the possibility to express ideas, concepts, beliefs and meanings within accepted and consensual moral and ethics, without being afraid of your life".

In a relationship there should be freedom to express feelings and have conversations on a level that leads to development, thriving and transcending energy rather than harsh, angry, vicious discussions and yelling. This could possibly lead to physical and emotional violence/ abuse.
Freedom in a relationship means that openness is present, that meaningful listening is a virtue, and the dialogue is on equal terms in which dialectics is a goal. That means, that new knowledge and consciousness through the dialogue is forming both of you in a non-egocentric way. Helping and supporting your partner by meaningful listening, acceptance, and awareness means that you must step back, and let yourself be a sanctuary for your partner. This allows a common feeling that you both contributed to the outcome.
Freedom in the conversation is important because it means you don't have to be afraid of your partner's

reaction as you already know that she/he will listen meaningfully to what you have to say. Remember, freedom is not being able to behave in a vicious way and call the partner names. Accusing the partner or being condescending, as a kind of behavior will only lead to a defense mechanism in which the attacked part feels locked in what she or he is accused for. Such action is a misuse of freedom in an egocentric and narrow-minded way that only has one agenda and that is yourself.
If you take a moment and think about freedom in a relationship, you will find that it is essential if you want it to develop, thrive, last and even exist. Altruism is a key word, and so is meaningful listening.

When I met Monica, I felt her immense need to speak of things that she was unable to talk to anyone about, because she was afraid to be judged, as she had been in her earlier life. For her to be able to do that was a release of dimensions for her – she finally found someone that she trusted, felt safe with, but most of all listened to her in a meaningful non-judgmental and curious way. Until she found me, she had to write all her love down in a journal as a substitute for not being able to find a person that she could actually release it to, and even have deep and meaningful conversation with.
I listened to Monica as she released her love, affection and generosity, making sure that she felt secure, wasn´t

judged, that humor was a part of it and commented in between making sure that she was understood. I had the genuine curiosity and interest in what she told me. That's the freedom I gave her, allowing her to grow. This lead us to have even deeper conversations which took our relationship to another level where love began to occur.

To be able to love is freedom.

Love

Knowing that your love kept me alive before you even knew me

Monica

Love

Monica

My darling, I have dreamt of a love that you give me daily... I have searched for it my entire life and here you are.

I have always known from an early age in my childhood that I was different. My thoughts on love and life were always so deep and too intense. I always knew that if I put out my love like a beacon of light that it would be bright enough for someone to find me...the one that would understand my heart.

Many have tried to understand my love, but they have always said that it was too deep, and they could not connect or that they were afraid of such a love because it was "too real".

I love "love". I love... that is just what the fuck I do... I love people! Even at times when they are not in line with my love walk or my love talk. I always thought that I could love enough to bring light to their dark. For many people it is hard to love when they don't know how to love. But does anybody ever really know "how to love"?

Love is the action to love someone. Love is a solid thing. This is the union that "love" was built on. So as young children we are taught how to love by those around us and the environment. Our parents are our first teachers however, I still feel that deep down inside we are not the products of our environment. I say this because the soul at birth is pure and innocent and we have this innate sense of how to love that ultimately leads us. Not every home has loving parents and so we think that we are going to grow up and be fucked up to never have decent relationships. This could be true, however there are people out there that may have said "You know, I was not loved or was not shown love as a child and I swore I was not going to be that way when I grow up". I have known many people to grow up in an environment that didn't have love, yet some of the most loving people came out of those situations to share their love with the world.

I believe that when we are born, the love of our lives is out there because we are created from cosmic stardust together. As I sit here and type, the tears flow down my cheeks because when I think about it... when I was born...my darling Jørgen, you were already here waiting for me and you didn't even know it.

You see, when I was 5 years old, I dreamt about you and I loved you. I loved you so much that I know with my soul that I brought you to me. I "loved you" to me! I lived my life in such a way that I gave love to everyone so that when it was time to collide with you I would see that our "love energy" would mesh and vibrate at a dimension like never before. It would be different, it would feel different and it truly does.

Love is powerful and healing. I know that you were out there when I was sick...and because of the love that I have for you, that I was going to survive so that I could show you love, give you love. Love brought me back from death. I know that everything I have gone through I survived because of the love I have in my heart for you that I put out to the Universe and the love that you have in your heart was preparing you for me. I know that your love is what kept me alive before you even knew me. That is how powerful love is. There was no doubt...our paths were going to cross at some point. Not to mention, that love is so precise that it brought two hearts together through music across an ocean from around the world together...yeah, I would say that is some pretty powerful love!

As I said, I love "love" so much that I teach and help people find that love inside of themselves and in their relationships no matter what kind. Because we all deserve to have the love and relationships we want, need, crave.

So many people just give up without stepping back to see how love can move in their lives deeper than the superficial way that they are used to. True love is far from superficial....and it is my mission in this life to show the world that.

Love never gives up...because I never gave up loving the one that is my Cosmic Supernova, the one who is made of the same cosmic stardust as I am... that is you, my darling. Love does not allow you to give up because it gives you the courage and the strength to go each day and try again even when it looks like it is impossible. It gives you the courage and the strength to do things you never thought were possible. Love gives you comfort and peace in times when things are unbearable. Love is forgiving when there is a misunderstanding....and you feel the embrace of love to melt the anger away. Love is reassuring when that embrace is felt to know that things will be ok. It holds your hand when you are scared.
Love does not judge the color of your skin, the tone in your voice, the shape of your body or the place you were born. Love never ends as it is infinite even after death it remains through your legacy to your children, grandchildren... and we are once again united in the cosmic stardust from where we were created... together in another state... another realm and still in love.

The power of love can fill a void so deep that even if a room looks empty with only me sitting there... that room is full of love that radiates just from my soul so that anybody that walks in will be able to feel it in my embrace, see it in my eyes as they sparkle. My thoughts and feelings for you radiate outward for the world to see, so the emptiness around me truly does dissolve.

When you are in love, you trust the other person with your soul, your heart and there will be no mis-understandings because loving someone so deeply, you would never want to hurt them or give them any doubt. True love does not allow that. Nor does it allow pain, confusion, or heartache.

I crossed an ocean and found love. On the inside of love, I found affection and devotion, admiration, and protection. I found in this love also strength, courage, inspiration, creation, passion, sensuality, and seduction, but most of all I found a beautiful soul that gives me space to be my true authentic self. I found in this love a man that loves me for me... FOR ME!

In my 46 years I have never seen someone with love in their eyes for me the way I see it in his. His eyes show a love that words are not needed from him to say that he loves me...I can see it, feel it, once again...the voice of "the silent warrior". I knew it before those words were spoken, this is how beautiful his soul is. His love is so pure and powerful that all the pieces of my heart that had ever been broken and I had tried to put back together, he put his hand on my heart and secured them. He spoke life back into my life.

I love my life, my friends, my family so much. My son is my biggest fan, and I am his. I lived my life for my son so he could see my love on display as I was his example. And now I love my life even more because I am in love with the one that takes my breath away daily, the one that gives me space to be vulnerable and silly, serious and always lets me speak incessantly...and never judges me. I finally found my warrior to love in depths that he is not afraid to meet me in as we swim in oceans of conversations, diving into emotions and vulnerability holding hands as we float back to the surface. A true warrior, he is.
I finally found a place in love that I can be... just be.

Jørgen

I am really overwhelmed in the way Monica describes her love for me. I guess it is because she never had love the way she found in me, but there is really nothing special about me – I just love her.

In my perspective, love as a holistic being does not exist, as love requires vibrant energy from the ones who experience it, otherwise there will be no experience of love. So, if we assume that love only exists through the energy that creates it, it is my perception, that that energy comes in many different forms. It is a bit of a paradox because it co-exists as an immanent deeply felt emotion, that at the same time is radiated outward as an acknowledgement to and from another loving energy. That interaction of love-energy is not a boring circle of life, it is a growing spiral. A spiral that binds the energies together, so that they in co-existence can join forces, get even stronger and take them to a higher tier of love. At that tier, love becomes a phenomenon that can survive anything even where death as the ultimate destruction of love, is not even regarded as a fear. When death occurs, you are still in love and give love.
The energies of love can exist everywhere, and as human beings we are all deep down capable of feeling and showing it, even though it sometimes seems so hard or inconceivable. We are all given the possibility to show and feel it from when we are born.

Love is constantly on its way as a dynamic force that is able to reassure, give comfort, give affection, give devotion and connect, but it doesn´t fight evil, it doesn´t have to, because they can´t co-exist – when love is

present, evil will dissolve - it can´t exist.
Love can be a realm of beauty in itself, but it needs to be kept alive or reappear in another form consisting of new energies in order to create itself.

If you met love while walking down the street you would probably see it stroll along with its friends, who on the inside of love might be "affection and devotion", and on the outside might be "admiration and protection". Love has many other friends and they probably will be nearby with "inspiration" talking to "creation" at the corner, "aesthetic" having a beer with "passion" at the bar, and "seduction" having dinner with "beauty" at the local restaurant. Meanwhile "disclamation" is confirmed by "victimhood", "evil" is deported by "justice and truth" and "indolence" does not stand a chance holding hands with life.

Love can even exist at an empty spot because emptiness will reflect your thoughts from the nothing to everything. Meaning that love can be created from your own mind as a reflection against the emptiness proving that emptiness will dissolve, and a form of love will now exist in an immanent state ready to radiate and connect. When you're in love there is no doubt, - love cannot co-exist with doubt.

I love my son so much, that I become vulnerable when I talk about him, because I miss him and have missed him my whole life due to a physical distance. So my love is shown through tears in my eyes – the tears of love and happiness because I have him.
I'm in love with a beautiful soul. She allows me to be who I am, and actually loves me because of who I am. That is a rare thing, but you know when it is there.

I'm in love with life because of the above.

Emptiness

Is solid ground for growth

Jørgen

Emptiness

Monica

So many people walk this earth and just exist, numb to everything around them. For some they are truly empty, past running on fumes, so they adapt and just become... numb.

Emptiness can mean different things for everyone. For some, emptiness is being completely drained of all emotions, for others it could be that they are alone, introverted. I think one of the worst feelings of emptiness is being in a relationship and feeling so alone, unheard, unloved and so empty that you feel like you are withering away. But, if only you had that one touch, loving word, you would begin to fill your soul again.

When I met Jørgen, I think I was one of those people that smiled on the outside, but I was so empty even though I had come a very long way. I have given to everyone and everything in my life every bit of me. I am a giver by nature and although I had learned my lessons a long time ago to set my boundaries, there was still that part of me that would give until I was bone dry, void of all emotions to the point that I would become physically sick. My check engine light was constantly on. My soul was never really quite ever full and at times just ran off of fumes.

I was one of those people that adapted to my environment and lived my life happily, but I would still cry myself to sleep every night... every single night. I felt so empty and would cry out to The Universe" I just needed someone to hear me... I just needed someone to hold me... I just needed someone to speak to me".
The pain in my heart was unbearable at times that I felt like my heart would literally stop at any given moment. Each day I got up and started out with so much life in me and as the day wore on, I gave to work, family, friends, my dogs, but by the end of it all I had nothing left. I just wanted to curl up into a ball in my bed and cry again.

It's funny how although I was so empty, that I never gave up. That emptiness pushed me to love myself because if I stopped loving myself then my internal soul light would go dim and how would Jørgen see me. I mean seriously, I was already at a disadvantage that he was on the other side of the world and I didn't know it yet. I had to push through that intense emptiness and fill my own soul. I needed to not only fill my void but overflow it. I wanted him to see me, be curious of what he saw and fall in love, as I was already in love with him.

So many people get lost in their emptiness. They don't embrace it and use it for their advantage. They sit in the dark and wallow in it. We do not have to depend on others to fill us. It is at those times that we can use it as a learning tool. To reflect as to how we got to this point. Where did this all start? What is it we want that will fill us? For me, it was just to be heard... so simple... just hear me. I say it is so simple to just hear me and yet my whole life I went unheard. Yes, of course people listen to me when they seek me out for love advice, counseling, work... etc... but my soul and my heart were not heard in my personal life.

In relationships we have to ensure that our partners are full at all times. The two most important parts to that is to fill them with what they need from us, but also to ensure that they fill themselves with what they need. This does not mean we do all the work for them. It means that, in our love for them we must ensure they are doing things they love to do for example. Again, I cannot stress enough that this is different for everyone, it is not cookie cutter.

This all ties in with being vulnerable and speaking what it is you need to say your partner. If you don't communicate this, the emptiness grows, and the relationship starts to breakdown and can lead to breakups and divorce. Everything is connected and goes hand in hand. We can use vulnerability to fill the void of emptiness and we can use that emptiness to be vulnerable.

As I stated, when I met Jørgen I had been through so much the past 5 years, from being at death's door, going through a divorce, starting over from ground zero, packing up my life and moving, to my mom having a stroke, heart attack and cancer - all in one year, not to mention work, my radio show and my dog rescue. I was not only empty, but I was exhausted and very sick. Some days I was barely functioning. But I was so scared for my light to completely go out. I fought daily to embrace the dark. I talk about that through this book about embracing the dark side because it is in the darkness that we can see clearer, everything is magnified. Each day was another step upward from my sickness, more on that later when I talk about fear. It took 5 years to come out of being so sick that I know happened because of what I was feeling and lack thereof. So, when Jørgen came into the picture, the very day we spoke on the phone he gave me what I was looking for my whole life. He "heard me". He heard not just my words, but he heard my heart, he heard my soul and he reached out across the ocean and through time to touch me and hold me. He literally opened up the floodgates to my spirit and flooded me with love, compassion, joy, peace, inspiration, serenity, but most of all life. I thought I was in a good place after the past 5 years, but what was missing he filled in. Not only did he do that for me, but he reminds me daily to do what is good for me so that I do not find myself empty from giving to the world once again.

It is vital to be partners so that you can invest in each other and the relationship. It is also important to respect the other person if they need some space to do their own investing in themself. Don't take offense if they say "Hey, I just need a bit to breathe and reflect alone". So many times people take offense that they are not wanted or needed, but what is misunderstood is that some people just need to fill their own tank, this is the part I was talking about in self-care. Instead of chastising them for needing some space, step back and hold space for them. That right there is one of the most precious and beautiful things someone can do for you... hold space while you retreat, heal, fill, and renew.

Use the emptiness as a force to push you to the other side. Use it to not settle for just anybody that will drain you further, but for someone that will gladly pour into you. Use it to reach for what you want in this life so that it does not happen again. Don't get lost in emptiness to the point where you are too weak and just become numb to this beautiful world and life that you were put here to lead.

Despite that he gives me so much, there is still a side of emptiness that I have that will remain until I am physically in his arms. Energetically he wraps me in his love, but we are still in the middle of a lockdown and I cannot get to him physically. So, there is a part of me that still feels a bit empty until I am wrapped in his arms and him in mine. Physical emptiness is real. We are all wired to be affectionate and show it to our partner. I remember being sick in the hospital and not knowing if I was going to live or die. I was lost in my emptiness, but I used it to push me to live... I needed to find my love and 5 years later I did.

Every day I am so full of gratitude for Jørgen and his constant, unselfish outpour of love and support that not only fills me but keeps me overflowing.

Jørgen

It is hard to hear that Monica had been giving so much her whole life, and yet she was getting nothing back, except from her son. The consequences are obvious – you just wear out your body and your soul – the light disappears. So, to be able to fight against the odds and using the darkness and emptiness to come back, is astonishing. I am truly happy that I was able to ignite her light again.

Emptiness is a concept that has different meanings to different people. Some might consider emptiness as scary in the sense of being lost, alone, isolated or even trapped in monotone thoughts. While others might see the emptiness as an opportunity to retreat, gain new energy, empty the mind for thoughts or find yourself in a world, that accelerates so fast, that it is hard to keep up.
What I´m curious about is, what is there in the entrance to emptiness? Imagine you are standing in the entrance to emptiness – what do you see? Is it dark or light, is it heavy or light, what expectations comes in mind? I guess it depends on the person who stands there, and if being there is voluntary, compulsory or is the feeling of being trapped.
Being at the entrance to emptiness to me is a privilege because at that moment you can decide how to use the emptiness – you do have a choice - the choice of letting nothing help you.

In my opinion emptiness is a void where you can display, challenge, review, analyze, evaluate and transcend your thoughts. It may sound peculiar that the emptiness in itself can be a powerful constructive force. It is the substance of the emptiness itself which apparently seems like nothing that hides the latent energy which is

stored in nothing.
Nothing can be extremely helpful, which sounds highly remarkable, but if you think about it, nothing is actually everything – how so? Well if there is nothing, then nothing is something, and therefore everything. You will find that if you use the emptiness in a constructive way, you can play against nothing and in return gain everything or at least something – because nothing will never judge you. Emptiness is also an oxymoron, because the attributes to emptiness is nothing and the insignificance to emptiness is also nothing. So, the attributes to emptiness, is how it is perceived by the being who is looking at it or experiencing it.

What is in the empty spot or place? I don´t have the answer, so my answer will be as good as yours. The point is that thinking about it is a powerful and reflective exercise even though it can be difficult to comprehend.

I find it particularly important that emptiness exists in a relationship and used as a tool to reinforce the love and the attraction. Being nothing together and individually, is an essential part of being everything to each other.
So… practice nothing to obtain everything.

I felt Monica's emptiness the first time I saw one of her quarantine videos. I saw the vulnerability, the longing she had to open her heart, and when she did, I have held it dearly ever since - and still do.

Vulnerability

Like a dish of ice cream on a hot summer´s day,
I melt into you

Monica

Vulnerability

Monica

The mere concept of writing about vulnerability is a bit scary and indeed puts you in an open place of vulnerability... but how fucking freeing is that? It can be very liberating, more on that in just a bit!

It was the sincerity and the vulnerability along with strength that I saw in your eyes that captured me. I felt like the vulnerability that you tried to hide was there for me to see and match mine. We are both strong, yet there is a certain side to us that only a few can see even through the layers of protection we put up.

Before I speak about being liberated through vulnerability, let me just say that I love you and I trust you....so with that said darling, I am able to be my true authentic, open, emotional, scared, powerful, free spirit, vulnerable me.

I have always been the strong one. The one that people would come to in their time of being vulnerable, but I was never granted that in return as most would hold that against me. I was never able to let myself go in any aspect. For me, to be vulnerable is to peel the layers off of me in all places in my life, work, relationships, friends, etc.

It was not that I was intimidated to show that side, it was that many people did not understand where I was coming from or it was just too deep for them, much like how I love.

I think for the most part there must be a huge trust that I must have to share that part of me... and guess what, you are the one I trust completely. I have been able to peel my layers off like comfortably undressing in front of you, ready to bare it all. You have never judged me for that. Instead you opened your arms and told me that it was ok to take that deep sigh of relief... and I did. Thank you for that.

I am not afraid to cry in front of you or say the stupidest things because you will comfort me through my tears and laugh with me when I get my German cities mixed up or tell you about that one time I totally forgot to put the color in the developer to color my hair! For once in my 46 years I finally feel free... liberated and have come out from behind my black shroud of protection. You lifted the veil to see my true light. And even though I am pasty pale from those covers, when you pulled that back from off of me, I will admit that it felt so good. I was free and you were there smiling and encouraging me. Just as I do with you.

When I work with couples that drift apart it is mostly because they lack that part in their relationships to trust the other person with their most deep feelings. It can be hidden with "Obsessive Compulsive Behavior", or a rigid and very structured environment. It could also be from our upbringing that we do not know how to be vulnerable as that shows weakness. When we show that side of our self it takes extreme courage. When I see couples that condemn their partner for showing raw authenticity it is heartbreaking. We must be there to listen and to be that sounding board for the other person. We don't always have to respond or speak, sometimes the most important part is just to be present and listen....to hold space for that person. We should never judge our partner or anybody for that matter, for letting their guards down to release. When we do that, we start that domino effect of neglect of our partner and the decaying of that union, the bond, the relationship. I get it, we have been through past hurts, traumas and we are afraid to go through that again, but if we hold everything in, or if we do not allow ourselves to let go, we go down a very dark rabbit hole.

I have been in relationships where my feelings, my words, my thoughts, my ideas, my work, my life meant nothing to my partner. I got lost in work and my rescue (I rescue pit bulls), at least my dogs would listen to me.

I see so many couples in trouble because one is too needy, but I don't like to use that word "too needy". They are needing to be validated and express themselves. They are needing to release those words, emotions, thoughts, ideas, creativity, sexual passion, intimacy, and they are rejected or turned away. It is difficult for both sides. The one that rejects may not know how to be vulnerable due to their childhood or something they have been through that they have a wall up. It is difficult for the one wanting to show that vulnerable side, but when they are turned away with a cold shoulder, they can sometimes become numb to it and just settle for the "status quo", but does it have to be that way? No, it does not. Again, the most important part about being vulnerable is trust. We have to trust that we will not be shamed, condemned, ridiculed, judged, belittled, laughed at, shut down, rejected, abandoned and once we have that trust you are now set free and how amazing that feels. Finally, finally you can move on in the relationship and evolve. There is nothing that can hold either of you back where peace surrounds you and love fills you. When I see couples go through this and find their way back from the brink of divorce it is such an honor to witness the melting of those souls.

To see someone so vulnerable is like seeing a beautiful masterpiece coming to life. Each word spoken so freely is a brush stroke on the canvas. Each thought and idea expressed as a shade of color. Each tear and laugh or emotion is a twist in the portrait. With that final sigh of relief, the signature at the bottom of the creation... which is your soul.

Not only is that a beautiful experience for someone to do that, but to be a witness is even more so. It takes courage and strength to let go and hope that the other person will not judge you, condemn you or turn away from you.

Right from the jump I felt like I could do that with Jørgen. He also gave me that courage and strength to show the sides of me that I would never show to anybody else. My stress and anxiety would never be shown to the world and yet it was like he felt it, saw it, and gave me space to unfold. That is the true essence of a warrior when he holds space for his goddess to heal, to express, to be free, safe, but mostly protected.

As humans we all deserve to have that sunlight of freedom shine on us. We deserve to be our raw and authentic selves especially with the one we love and trust. If we cannot be that, then why even be with that person? It is bad enough we must be out in the world strong for everyone. When we are with our loved one, the world melts away and the beauty of freedom comes in. As

Jørgen has said in the past to me" Freedom dances with beauty". Jørgen my love, you are my freedom.

With all this said, just know, my love, that I will always be there in return to listen, to embrace, to celebrate, to help you find the courage to be vulnerable with me, but most of all to protect you so you can be free to be the beautiful masterpiece that you are… just as you are for me.

Jørgen

You are right Monica, I couldn´t hide my shyness and vulnerability for you, and somehow I knew you would see it, because with your bare presence, you just gave me that security to open up – at least a little bit.

To write about the concept of vulnerability, makes me feel vulnerable in the sense of being intersubjective through emotions and openness. Even more so when speaking to a big audience that I don't know and can't see, yet at the same time it is a relief and a question of trust – but it's also very giving.

It is well known that being vulnerable in front of a person is more intimidating than if you were talking to the same person over the phone or if you wrote a letter. This is normally due to the fact that the things you want to talk about, will cause some emotional feelings expressed physically for example; crying, blushing, shaking, being scared of the reaction you will get and the fact that someone is watching you when you open up.

Normally people tend to hide their vulnerability in order to protect themselves and that's understandable, but at the same time they hide some of their beautiful soul, some of their humanity, some of their authenticity and some of their dignity. This may sound less charming, but it does not mean that you can´t be yourself. It´s just that you hide some of the real you. Of course, one should not open to everyone as there are degrees of vulnerability, and to whom which they are shown.
When I mention that you lose some dignity by not showing your vulnerability, it is because, there is no dignity in hiding the beauty of yourself - that´s a misunderstood attitude or belief.

If vulnerability has a purpose, it could be liberation – to be liberated from the things you struggle with alone or want the one you love to know about. To open and show your vulnerability, will cause a feeling of freedom. It´s a liberation of your mind and soul, and showing your vulnerability takes a lot of courage and strength, because

you´re actually sharing and giving some of your mind and soul to another person. Being vulnerable, is actually a big compliment, and not for the weak soul.
Usually many people think that showing their vulnerability, is a weak attitude, I have been like that for many years, but I have learned through time, that it is exactly the other way around, and that's a big relief.

When two people are sharing their vulnerability to each other it is not a fragile thing, it is a very strong commitment, trust, security, but most of all a transcending gift. When I use the term transcending in this context, I mean it as a catalyst for reaching a common concept, that might be more fragile or stronger than the two vulnerabilities as separate entities. Nevertheless it´s a new creation, a new perspective from which both individual and common development can occur.

I see vulnerability as a dynamic force, that has to be released at the right time to the right persons in order to obtain the mentioned liberation or freedom. You see, usually vulnerability's nearest friends are grief and sorrow as the good ones, and depression, stress, anxiety and unhappiness as the bad ones. If the vulnerability is not released or shown, the bad ones will take over and dominate which can lead to an unpleasant existence. When I distinguish between good and bad friends in relation to vulnerability, it is because sorrow and grief, even though they can feel very hard, they are usually a sign of love. The deeper the sorrow, the deeper the love.

When vulnerability meets with freedom it won't disappear. It will be protected by someone else besides yourself – and that gives a kind of comfort, that drives new energy from your mind and soul.

I still struggle with my vulnerability when I'm sharing my mind and soul, but in small steps I´m able to do it.
I´m vulnerable when I talk about my son, because I get tears in my eyes.
I get embarrassed when I want to show my feelings, and I will usually start to joke about things before I can open up and be real.

Fear

Don`t fear, fear itself –

fear for not being able to love

Jørgen

Fear

Monica

Anxiety, depression, worry, doubt, self-sabotage; just a few words that go along with fear. As humans we tend to let fear be the "cock blocker" in our lives. It holds us back from so much because we give it power...we feed it with our worry and our doubt. We make it more than it should be by letting it take over our soul, giving us a feeling of helplessness and distress. Sometimes we lay down and depression sweeps over us like a blanket of security in our misery, locked in the unknown abyss. Fear becomes such a comfortable place for us that we are afraid to not feel it.

Pretty scary when you look at it that way! Well, sadly that is what happens when we give fear power. When we let it take over and blind us, especially in relationships, new relationships, and those relationships that we want. I can't begin to tell you how many times I have been full of fear because of a new relationship or while I was in a relationship. What did I have to be afraid of? Myself? I never thought of being afraid of the other person, I was afraid of myself. Because of everything I had been through, I was afraid to be me. I was afraid that if they saw the true authentic me, then I would sink in the "my pity party...party of one"! I was always told that I was not good enough, thin enough, pretty enough, this enough or that enough and no matter how much healing you do, it can still creep back in every once in a while. I thought I had gotten away from all that nonsensical fuckery with my fears and anxiety, but it hit me once again. I thought I was done with all the self-doubt and fear, and for the most part I was, but I gave it power over me. As a result, I was not strong enough to fight through it and everything snowballed. I was too riddled with fear at this point and I was getting sick, actually let's just say "sicker".

When we let fear come over us, we become weak and cannot stand up for ourselves because we doubt everything, or we are so consumed with worry that we cannot see clearly. Sometimes we even become too accustomed to bad things happening to us because of our fear that bad things will happen. So, we walk around in fear of everything around us. We isolate ourselves and even settle for a relationship we know will not be amazing and allow you stay in your "box". The relationship is just status quo because you are ok with being locked in your fear, but hey, you are not alone. People come to me all the time with this issue. They are not satisfied in the relationship but will not leave it.

Sometimes, we even self-sabotage situations and relationships because we already know that it will not work out, or at least that is what we think because fear tells us that. Fear makes us think that we are not good enough for the person we are with and so we self-sabotage to avoid getting hurt. If we hurt our self-first, then it won't hurt as much. So many times, I have people that have come to me because they were so afraid of "what could be" instead of focusing on the "right now". They let fear drive their worry and anxiety and it pushes the other person away. Nobody wants a Negative Nelly around them.

What is worse is when other people project their misery and instill fear in us. Or, they remind you of your fears to hold you back. Instead of encouraging you and lifting you up, they point out and magnify them, and remind you of them, they use it as ammunition against us to break us down even more. Misery does love company, but here is the thing, you have to be aware of it and fight that dark side.

In relationships, it is vital that we are there to continue to love our partner unconditionally through their fears. It is important that we let them know that in their fears that they are not alone as we stand with them. We encourage them and hold their hand. Sometimes words are not even needed as it is just a matter of sitting next to them. I have never had unconditional love. To be loved without conditions.... such a foreign concept to me although I see it all the time with clients, so I know it is real. And now, I know it is real, because Jørgen gives me that, and by doing that he removes my fears.

Fear can be so many different things in relationships. Will it work out? Will he love me if I get sick? What about the distance? What about family? What about this or that? It is easier to just give into fear, so we don't get hurt. But what if we pushed past that fear, stayed positive and got to the other side of it and found a life of bliss? How fucking amazing would that be? When I sent him a friend request I knew where he was, but when your soul stops you and says... "That is him", you pay attention, and you don't even think of anything else. I sent him a friend request and even though he was not sure what I wanted, but I didn't let fear hold me back. I kept trying to keep that door open for him to come through. I didn't let fear hold me back from the love of my life despite that so many people think it is absolutely nuts to fall in love with someone on the other side of the world. SO, FUCKING WHAT! The heart does not measure distance....it just loves. And as I have said so many times already, I have loved him since I was 5 years old. I could tell he had fear in him and did not want to let himself love me even though he already did. I remember one night we were on one of our dates and I asked him if he was scared... he said "yes because of distance". I looked at him and said, "I understand and if you should walk outside your front door tomorrow, see a beautiful woman with a beautiful soul that captures your heart and lives in the same place for you to see every day, I will encourage it and be so happy for you". Even though, I knew in my heart that I would be so devastated because I love him, but at the same time, I could not hold him back. He gave me the gift of peace. My fear was put to ease when he looked me in the eyes and told me that he was not going anywhere. I just felt it in the very depth of my soul that he meant it; his eyes never lie. I tell him all the time that I am not afraid to love him through the miles and when you know that you are going home, how can you be afraid?!

It is human nature to hold ourselves back from something that we know might hurt us. Fear is a defense mechanism to either hurt us or protect us. But if we hold on to fear, we may never have that dream job that we are too afraid to go after, we may never have the relationship we want because we are stuck in fear that we are not good enough. Perhaps you hold yourself back from a life you envision but are too afraid to pack up and start over. You then lead a mediocre existence because fear holds you in captivity. The life I envision is one that is taking me across an ocean, to another part of the world where fear is nonexistent for me. All that we want is on the other side of fear. We just have to take that first step when we let go and allow ourselves to be brave.

Jørgen puts my fears to bed. He is so strong when I am having an off day. As I type these words my biggest fear is that I will not get to see him because we are on a lockdown and cannot travel. As much as I try to hide my fears, he knows me already and can see it behind my eyes, because my eyes never lie either. I am typically a positive person, but I felt so defeated and helpless as I cannot just jump on a plane to go see him. Yet, he sits on the other side of the screen and says, "No worries Nica, we will see each other". I have a history of an autoimmune disease and he has been so supportive and encouraging. When I am scared, he reaches through the miles and holds me, I can feel him. So many times, people leave their partners out to hang alone because they just can't be bothered, or they don't believe them. Fear is real and when you use it against your partner that is such cruelty. It is a form of emotional abuse. This goes for all relationships in which one person treats the other as such. If you love someone so much, how can you stand to see them tremble in fear? How can you stand by and watch them go down a rabbit hole of anxiety? Love does not allow that. Love fights all that and overcomes it. Love battles demons that wrestle with you in oceans of black sludge and brings you to safety.

In Jørgen, I find strength, courage, bliss, and the other side of my fears. He is the one that fights my nightmares before they get to me, the one that is my powerful silent warrior, the one that protects my soul from those that try to use fear against me.

Jørgen

I will always be there for you Nica – fear is merely a creation that amplifies itself, if we do not confront it and make it go away – and we will do that together.

When you talk about fear you have to include anxiety as well, because they go hand in hand. You could argue that they work in unison, affected by each other but expressed in different ways.
My distinction between the two concepts is that fear is something that occurs suddenly in a given situation, in which you have to react to it, whereas I see anxiety more as a long term condition of being scared which is unhealthy for both mental and physical health. Anxiety is often a condition on the premises of fear which can create an environment where it is easy to be provoked. If you choose to act like it is expected or wanted from you, it

often means that you will hide the real you, conceal your existence and lose yourself with devastating consequences.

When I read Monica´s perception of fear I got sad, as she is describing a fear for being herself. This is not because she doesn't like to be who she is. She has experienced a certain suppression and was unable to live her life as the person she is. Suppressed feelings can break any person.
In essence, if you have anxiety for your own existence and the behavior that it includes related to other people's dominance, influence, power, disrespect, or condescending behavior, then you have to break out of those relationships. If you remain in those types of relationships, you are contributing to your own dehumanization. This can damage your health all because you want to please other people so that you can avoid confrontation, where you go from anxiety into fear.

The interesting thing is, that in the gap or void between fear and anxiety there is a concept that fuels the relationship, which is hope – hope of a change, so you can be yourself, and show love as you want to show it. Quite possibly this might not happen. It is a naïve kind of hope, but sadly in many situations, that is what´s left to hold onto.

If a union doesn´t allow you to communicate about your relationship and feelings, and the only thing that comes out of it is a reaction causing fear, you should leave that relationship.

As humans we seek a life without having to fear something and avoid anxiety if we can. In reality we will never be free of fear, it will always be there, but it´s how we handle the fear on a daily basis in our lives that matter. We can be afraid of too much responsibility, too much pressure, workloads, death, bad relationships, going through a divorce, scared to love, or showing emotions etc. and we must continuously muster the strength to live and fight the fear so that daily life is acceptable, or even better - joyful. Luckily, that is not that difficult for most people, because they have learned to control fear.
To be able to control fear you have to hold hands with it figuratively speaking. Even though, you don't want it in your life but by holding hands with fear, you know where it is at all time. You can control it and if you let go of it, it will control you.

I have fears too, but I have been able to control it for many years. I use fear to move on and get the strength to fight no matter what shows up. That does not mean, that I don't feel sad or anxious at times, but I hold hands with what causes it and that's why I am able to move on with fear in my hand, and the connection with fear is love.

I have had fear to:

- *love*
- *feel and show emotions*
- *to lose my beloved ones*
- *lose my job*

I still fear

- *to get praised (I want to hide)*
- *the worlds disturbing development*
- *to get a dangerous sickness*

But I do not let the fear take over, I use it to fight through love, and should it come to that – fight for real.

Remember by holding hands with your fear, you are showing it love. Even fear needs love. When it realizes that, it will be your friend - it will give you strength.

Devotion and sacrifice

I want to show him that in this devotion a beautiful life waits for not just me, but for us.

Monica

Devotion and sacrifice

Monica

Devotion - to be loyal, to love something or someone passionately. This can be positive and negative. It can take on two different realms depending on the person.

To be devoted to someone, to love them can be so incredibly beautiful. A life of devoted love for someone that your soul connects with is what we all want in this lifetime. It is rare but still possible. I have witnessed it myself with my grandparents. For 56 years they were so in love and devoted to each other. There is nothing that my grandfather would not do for my grandmother. He loved telling us his story of how he first saw her and said, "I am going to marry her and love her forever". And so, he did. It was one of the most beautiful love stories to be a witness to. His love and devotion for her was unconditional and limitless. She was perfect in his eyes. I wanted to have that kind of love and devotion when I grew up. I wanted to feel that when I was looked at by my beloved wherever he was, whoever he was. I was excited to know that I would have that. I watched their love through the years until his death, where even in his last breath he looked at her.

Some people may see devotion as a sign of weakness or being subservient. That is not the case when a person is so in love that they want to do good things for the other person out of a place of love to see them happy. You will do anything and everything to see them smile to ensure that they never know pain or hurt. This is where sacrifice comes in, because to love so intensely does not come without sacrifice.

I grew up seeing my grandmother's devotion to my grandfather as well. She loved him so much and wanted him to have everything that she could give him of herself. In my culture we show our love and devotion by our actions and cooking. She enjoyed cooking for him and took such a pride in having his meals ready for him three times a day, not because he had her like that and demanded that of her, but because she wanted to do that for him. He worked and she was a homemaker that wanted to devote her life to her family. She raised five children, took care of a household and a husband. I loved helping her cook for him. I wanted to grow up and do the same. You can say they were my role models. To see her joy as she cooked for him and presented his meal and to see his eyes light up...it truly was magical. You are probably thinking, "Monica, this was just a woman cooking a meal for her husband", but what you are missing if you ask me that, is the fact that to see the love between them and each action between them was true devotion to each other. So, something so simple can mean so much. This was her devotion.

Sacrifice could be to give something up, for something else that they feel would be better. For some they will sacrifice a life they knew to be with someone they love just to have a lifetime of devotion with their soulmate. When it comes to devotion and sacrifice, they are holding hands. Life is not always perfect and sometimes, as I stated you may have to sacrifice something to have the love of your life, which is worth it because love like this is not something you see or feel every day.

When I am working with couples, I can see how in their relationships they have become selfish. Selfish with themselves and no longer is it about the couple but about the individual. The devotion to each other is no longer there. In the beginning, when we choose that person to go out with, to date, we know that we want to continue in the relationship to see where it goes. We devote time to them and show love to them. For some, they sacrifice time to travel to see them or to stay awake to talk to them. But it is worth it when again as previously stated, it is for a chance at true love. When couples lose that devotion to each other, it opens the door for them to drift apart. They become so consumed on the selfishness that it is almost a "demand" that the other person does things that they once did out of love, not to mention those things can also be taken for granted. Those acts are no longer special when there is a demand or expectation. Devotion loses its luster and magic. When selfishness replaces devotion and sacrifice, it can turn a relationship sour and turn a couple against each other. Devotion and sacrifice are quite the opposite of selfishness as it is selfless. We want our partners to be so happy, joyful, full of peace and love that we will do anything for them. We will hold their hearts in our hands like fine china to ensure that it never breaks. Sometimes couples lose sight of this and have to find their way back to each other because again, in the beginning we are devoted to them so much so, that when there is a proposal it is because you don't want them to be with anybody else but you and you with them.

Some people see sacrifice as a bad thing. "You sacrificed your life to move across the world?". But how is that a bad thing when it is for the person you love and want to spend the rest of your life with? It is not a bad thing when something so amazing waits for me. So many people lose sight of this because their fear holds them back. It all ties in together. A beautiful life waits on the other side of fear. An amazing life waits on the other side of sacrifice because I am not giving up anything, I am actually gaining the world, because he is my world.

The flip of all this is, is when devotion turns to the negative side. When devotion leads to pain and suffering. You devote your life to someone or something that may exhaust you and drain you as you sometimes feel as if you are chasing something that you can never have. It can lead to depression, anxiety, anger, hopelessness, exhaustion and even a feeling of failure. To devote and sacrifice life and love for something or someone with no return can also lead to a deep feeling of desperation. It becomes unhealthy. At some point the sacrifice must be made to cut the tie to something that hurts us instead of gives us joy. In this instance the devotion is unhealthy, but the sacrifice once again is what will take us to the other side of peace.

With Jørgen I am totally devoted to him. People that know me, see this in me. They see my devotion and that I will go to the ends of the earth for him. I want to spend the rest of my life showing him love and holding his heart in my hands so that it never breaks. I want to show him that in this devotion a beautiful life waits for not just me, but for us.

"I´m hopelessly devoted to you" Olivia Newton John sang, and those who have seen Grease, might remember her outcry for love to someone, who put her love aside. Well I am hopelessly devoted to Nica, and I do have her love.

When you're in love with someone, who doesn't love you back and you still are devoted to the person, you could argue that devotion can be hopeless, when your feelings are not requited. On the other side, it proves, that devotion can be so strong, that it overcomes mutual love, and that kind of devotion could be regarded as a sacrifice, because even though your love or feelings are not requited, you still have the strength to stand by what you feel, despite the hurting it may create.

Both devotion and sacrifice are important in a relationship. To be devoted demands sacrifice, and actually the two concepts are synonyms. If you look at the root of devotion, it also means some kind of sacrifice.

In the modern and postmodern world, devotion is normally perceived as a loving gesture where you give yourself to another person. To give oneself can be in many different relations, and usually it means to sacrifice something, but that does not necessarily have to be a bad thing. For example, most people are devoted to their family, and therefore they will help them financially, help them move, or just be there in hard times. Even though it's a sacrifice in time, money, energy or social contact, it´s a sacrifice you probably are more than willing to give, just like when you do something nice for the one you're in love with. You do that, because it makes you happy to see your loved one happy.

The good thing about being devoted is that even though you sacrifice something, you also benefit from that sacrifice by seeing the ones you gave it to become happy and thankful. The best part of being devoted is when you feel the devotion is returned.

The headline "Devotion and Sacrifice" is actually a paradox because the two concepts deep down mean the same. We just use the concept of devotion in another context today. Even though sacrificing something immediately sounds like a negative action, it does not have to be. Being able to sacrifice and give in to another person, is a very strong and mature character that symbolizes altruistic behavior in order to make other people feel good.

Devotion seen from that perspective gives it a glory of non-egocentrism and shows that if you possess that ability and that character, you will probably be perceived as a person with a big heart, someone authentic, genuine and altruistic. Someone to be trusted, but most of all, someone that has the qualities to be in a relationship – because love is not for free, it is created by mutual devotion in a positive context.

Epilogue

Monica

As I sit here, I can't help but have tears running down my face as I come to the end of this journey of writing this book with Jørgen. I cry because it has been quite the journey indeed.

Throughout this process of writing "Things I Needed To Say", I have found myself. I have truly shed many skins and allowed myself to be the most vulnerable I have ever been. It was effortless for me to do that. The very first conversation we had, my walls were down, my guard was thrown out the window, my heart was wide open, ready to give him love and receive his, and my soul was finally at peace.

I had been walking in the dark my whole life to protect myself from judgement. I walked in the dark so that nobody could see my bruises, my heartache, my pain, my tears. I walked in the dark because that is where I was told to be as nobody would love me for me, so I had to hide. I hid Monica because she was too much for most people. In the dark you really could not see me, you only saw what I allowed.

On April 4th, 2020 Jørgen came into the dark with me and flashed his light. He held out his hand and as terrifying as it was to be seen, it was also the most liberating. I was so exhausted mentally, emotionally, spiritually, and physically. His hand was so strong he lifted me out of my shadow and allowed me to put my face up to the sun and take a huge, deep sigh of relief with my arms stretched wide open.

For once in my entire 46 years of life, I was seen, heard, validated, comforted, and loved. I could feel the sun on my face, the breeze on my skin and hear his voice bring me back to life.

Throughout this journey of writing this book I have bared myself to him in ways that I would never have ever dreamed of with anybody else. He woke up that side of my goddess that I had feared been put to sleep forever, but each piece that I wrote was truly inspired by Jørgen. Every word on these pages came from a place of immense love and desire for him, respect and honor for him, inspiration because of him. Everything that I have said on these pages were things that I have never wanted to say to anybody else and now I know why, because these words were meant for him and him alone.

For the record, in case you are wondering, there are places on these pages where I have called him my "Cosmic Supernova". That is because I truly believe with all my heart that he is not only my soulmate, but that he and I are made of the same cosmic stardust that even through the miles we were drawn back together. He is epically cosmic....and powerful so much that as a supernova he enveloped me in his arms and consumed me once again to be as one.

On this journey, he has given me grace when I stumble, passion to wake me up, intimacy in all aspects, understanding when the world couldn't make sense of me, compassion when I would just cry and bawl my eyes on days when work was stressful, I wasn't feeling good or just because I need to spill over. He has given me peace in times of unrest and protection while I sleep. But most of all, he has given me and shown me true unconditional love, no limits, no boundaries, just pure unconditional love.

What you have read on these pages are our hearts and actual conversations that we have had as we have grown and still grow to know each other. You have read our love story, watched it unfold, unravel, and become more and more cosmic. You have watched our love and communication and how it has evolved from poetic longing, to poetic foreplay. It truly is a beautiful poetic conversation... all because of the things I needed to say...

****At the time these poetic conversations were written, we have not met physically. I am still in Texas like a trapped rat and he remains in Denmark because of COVID-19 and all the borders are locked for International Travel. We still meet each other daily, have our time together and plan to see each other as soon as borders open again for travel without quarantine on either side. We had several different times planned, but borders were locked spring, summer and now fall 2020. In my heart I know that it will happen sooner rather than later. My flight has been booked and all travel arrangements have been made for 2021. I know that when I see him face to face and not behind a screen, I will melt into him because he truly is my Cosmic Supernova and the poetic conversations will continue on... stay tuned...*

I will close with these words.

It was under the stars where my soul first whispered your name. It is under these same stars where I sit and thank The Universe for your existence and the stars that led you to me. It is under these beautiful stars, my beloved, that I gaze upon where I have peace knowing you gaze upon them too even in our absence from each other.

It is under these stars, where my heart beats for you, where my eyes close and your name will be forever upon my lips. It is under these stars where you and I will embrace soon and finally The Goddess will be with her Warrior... forever your Moon Goddess.
Monica.

Jørgen

It has been an epic journey to write this book with Monica. It is our thoughts and conversations about relationships converted into a publication which we hope will inspire and motivate the readers.

The concepts we describe in Part 2, we see as the 8 fundamentals which is deeply connected, and it will always be a life accomplishment to work with them.

In Part 1 I chose to reply in a poetic way to the things Monica needed to say. I did that to show her how a response could be lifted to another dimension in which life and existence can be portrayed from a different perspective and thereby facilitate openness.

Our book is finished and now I cannot wait until I will see Nica in 2021. I imagine how it will be like when I meet her in Copenhagen Airport, when I will look in to her eyes for real, hug and caress her, kiss her and wipe away tears of joy from her cheek.

I will end this with a poem –

When I meet you - that I already met

See you in real life I will be paralyzed
even though I know you I will be surprised
breathtaking, joyful, and mesmerized – feelings
everything and nothing will reveal the meanings

You come from far away and yet you say home
I promise I will give you attention – you won't be alone

Jørgen